The RVers Road Atlas: Discover America's Safest RV Routes, Scenic Stops, and Campgrounds with Turn-by-Turn Navigation for Rural Roads, Real Detours, and Stress-Free Planning – With Easy-to-Read Maps

Daniel & Mariah Redwood

Table Of Contents

Your Road, Your Rules

There's something timeless about the open road—the promise of what lies beyond the next bend, the stillness of a mountain sunrise, or the salty air rolling in from the coast. Whether you travel by motorhome, trailer, camper van, or fifth wheel, one thing is certain: RVing isn't just a mode of travel—it's a lifestyle built on freedom, discovery, and the quiet joy of the journey itself.

This *RV Road Atlas* was designed with that spirit in mind. It's more than just a book of directions. It's a curated guide through some of the most scenic, iconic, and inspiring highways in North America—routes like the **Great River Road**, **Pacific Coast Highway**, **Going-to-the-Sun Road**, and **Skyline Drive**, among many others.

Each section offers:

- **Turn-by-turn navigation-style directions**, written clearly and faithfully to the classic routes
- **Scenic highlights and points of interest** worth pulling over for
- **RV-friendly campgrounds** chosen for both convenience and beauty
- **Fuel stops** that accommodate larger rigs and offer reliable access

This guide is for those who love slow travel. For people who want to park beside a cliff, cook dinner to the sound of waves, or wake up beneath the redwoods. It's built for planners and wanderers alike—those who want a little structure, but still leave room for the unexpected.

Let's roll.

Map Disclaimer

The maps in this book have been simplified and stylized to enhance clarity and usability for RV travelers. They are designed to highlight major scenic routes, cities, and points of interest rather than provide detailed turn-by-turn navigation. For precise, real-time directions, road conditions, or local traffic updates, we recommend using a GPS device or official navigation app during your journey.

All base maps are derived from **OpenStreetMap** and are used under the **Open Database License (ODbL)**.

⚙ How to Use This Book

Each Route is Divided by Day: Routes are organized into **daily driving segments**. Each "Day" includes the total distance, estimated driving time, and a recommended stopping point, often in or near a scenic town, park, or campground. **Clear, Turn-by-Turn Directions:** You'll find **step-by-step driving instructions**, just like a GPS — but more reliable in remote areas. Each turn is numbered and includes road names, distances, and helpful context (e.g., landmarks, changes in terrain). **Campgrounds & Overnight Suggestions:** Each day includes a list of **RV-friendly campgrounds** with locations, notes on amenities, and approximate distance from the starting point. You'll find both public parks and private RV sites, with options for different budgets and rig sizes. **Easy-to-Read Maps:** Each section features **simple, large-format maps** that give you a visual overview of the route. Use them to see the big picture, mark your progress, or follow along offline.

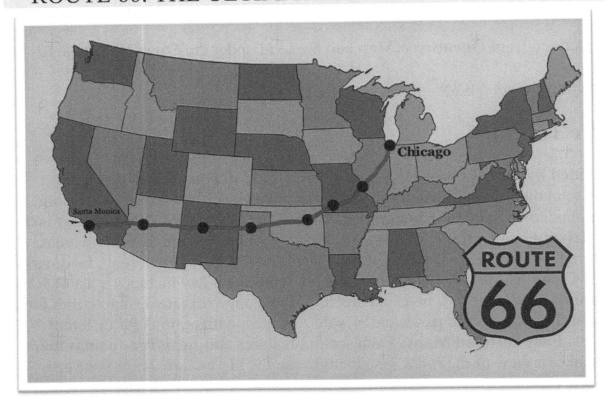

Route 66. The very name conjures images of open roads, vintage diners, and the spirit of the American dream. Stretching from **Chicago, Illinois, to Santa Monica, California**, this iconic highway covers **2,448 miles** and traverses eight states, each offering its own slice of history, charm, and adventure. It's not just a road—it's a journey through time, culture, and landscapes. The estimated fuel cost to complete the entire Route 66 in an RV ranges from **$300 to $400**, depending on fuel efficiency and gas prices along the route.

The Birth of Route 66

Route 66 was officially established on **November 11, 1926**, as part of the original U.S. Highway System. It connected **Chicago to Los Angeles**, creating one of the first **interstate highways** that allowed Americans to traverse the country with relative ease. During the **Great Depression**, Route 66 became a lifeline for thousands of families migrating westward in search of jobs and new beginnings. Immortalized in John Steinbeck's classic novel *The Grapes of Wrath* (1939), it became known as the **"Road of Flight"** for the Dust Bowl refugees escaping the devastated farmlands of the Midwest.

🚐 The Golden Age of Route 66

After World War II, Route 66 truly flourished. It became a major **commercial artery**, connecting small towns and big cities alike. As **automobile culture boomed** in the 1950s and 60s, the road became synonymous with **family vacations, roadside diners, and quirky motels**. The highway saw the rise of iconic stops like:

- **Cadillac Ranch (Amarillo, TX)** - An art installation of half-buried Cadillacs.
- **Wigwam Motels (Holbrook, AZ and San Bernardino, CA)** - Famous for their teepee-shaped rooms.

- **Blue Whale of Catoosa (OK)** - A whimsical roadside attraction and swimming spot.

Day 1 – From Historic Begin Route 66 Sign to Double J Campground

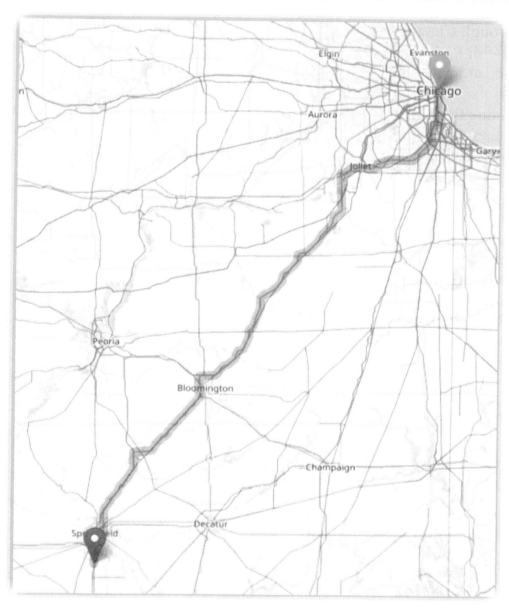

Your Route 66 journey officially kicks off in **Chicago**, where you'll find the iconic *"Begin Route 66"* sign at **East Adams Street**. As you navigate through the **Dan Ryan Expressway**, you'll pass through industrial corridors and rail yards—a reminder of Chicago's historical role as a transportation hub. After merging onto **I-57** and later **I-80**, the scenery becomes increasingly rural, with long, open stretches of farmland and small towns that evoke the golden age of American road trips. Once you connect to **I-55 South**, you're aligned with much of the original Route 66 alignment, passing through several classic roadside attractions and small communities like **Wilmington**, **Dwight**, and **Pontiac**—each offering nostalgic glimpses into Americana: vintage diners, antique gas stations, and Route 66 murals.

Directions:
Distance: 215 miles (346 km) – **Time:** 4:10

1. Start at the Historic Route 66 Begin Sign on E. Adams Street in Chicago and head west for 0.3 miles
2. Turn left onto S. Michigan Avenue, then right onto Jackson Boulevard and continue west for 0.5 miles
3. Merge onto Ogden Avenue (US-66 / US-34) and follow it through Cicero, Berwyn, Lyons, Brookfield, La Grange, Downers Grove, and Lisle for approximately 30 miles
4. Continue on Ogden Avenue through Naperville and Aurora, then follow Route 66 signage into Romeoville and turn onto IL-53 South toward Joliet for about 15 miles
5. From Joliet, continue south on IL-53 through Elwood and reach Wilmington, covering about 20 miles
6. Proceed through Braidwood, Godley, Gardner, and continue into Dwight along IL-129 and Old Route 66 for another 30 miles
7. Follow Old Route 66 south from Dwight through Odell and reach Pontiac, driving approximately 20 miles
8. Continue south through Chenoa, Lexington, and Towanda, entering Bloomington-Normal via Old Route 66 for about 35 miles
9. Proceed south from Bloomington through Shirley, Funks Grove, McLean, and Atlanta to reach Lincoln, covering another 40 miles
10. Drive from Lincoln to Springfield via Old Route 66, passing through Broadwell, Elkhart, and Williamsville for about 35 miles
11. Continue south through Leland Grove and Southern View and arrive in Chatham, driving approximately 10 miles
12. From Chatham, turn right onto Palm Road and continue for 2 miles
13. Arrive at Double J Campground, 9683 Palm Road, Chatham, IL 62629

Scenic Highlights & Points of Interest

Mile Marker	Location	Highlight
0 mi	Chicago, IL	Route 66 Begin Sign (78-98 E Adams St) – Iconic photo spot
2 mi	Lou Mitchell's Restaurant	Classic 1920s diner famous with Route 66 travelers
95 mi	Pontiac, IL	Route 66 Hall of Fame & Museum; Pontiac Oakland Auto Museum
120 mi	Normal, IL	Sprague's Super Service – restored 1930s gas station
160 mi	Atlanta, IL	Paul Bunyan Hot Dog Statue – quirky roadside Americana

| 200 mi | Springfield, IL | Lincoln Home National Historic Site, Cozy Dog Drive-In (birthplace of the corn dog) |

Rest Stops & Fueling

- **Pontiac, IL:** Ample fuel stations + local cafes
- **Bloomington/Normal, IL:** Large rest areas + RV-friendly gas stations
- **Atlanta, IL:** Small-town rest stop with parking

Overnight Stay Recommendation: Double J Campground & RV Park

9683 Palm Rd, Chatham, IL 62629 (Just south of Springfield)

Located ~200 miles from Chicago, this RV park offers full hookups (30/50 amp), pull-through sites, clean facilities, a pool, and easy access to Springfield attractions.

Rate: ~$40–$50/night
Phone: +1 217-483-9998
Website: doublejcampground.com

A clean, convenient stop perfect for Route 66 travelers.

Day 2 – From Double J Campground to Cuba, MO

Directions: Distance: 171 miles — **Time:** 3 hours and 17 minutes

1. Depart Double J Campground and head south on Palm Road for 2.1 miles.

2. Turn right onto Frazee Road and continue for 0.6 miles.
3. Turn left onto Old Route 66 and proceed for 0.1 miles.
4. Merge onto I-55 South via the entrance ramp and drive for 80.2 miles.
5. Keep left to continue on I-55 South/US-40 West for 0.7 miles.
6. Merge onto I-55 South/I-64 West/US-40 West and continue for 1.0 mile.
7. Keep right to stay on I-55 South/IL-3 South and drive for 1.6 miles.
8. Keep right to continue on I-55 South for 1.3 miles.
9. Keep right to merge onto I-44 West (Officer David Haynes Memorial Highway) and continue for 3.1 miles.
10. Continue on I-44 West (Officer Michael Barwick Memorial Highway) for 3.7 miles.
11. Continue on I-44 West (Police Officer Robert Stanze Memorial Highway) for 2.7 miles.
12. Continue on I-44 West (Police Officer Ernest M. Brockman Sr. Memorial Highway) for 3.7 miles.
13. Continue on I-44 West (Henry Shaw Ozark Corridor/US-50) for 68.4 miles.
14. Take exit 208 toward MO-19: Cuba, Owensville and drive for 0.3 miles.
15. Turn left onto MO-19 South and continue for 0.8 miles.
16. Turn left onto East Washington Boulevard (Historic Route 66) and proceed for 0.02 miles.
17. Arrive at your destination in Cuba, MO.

Stop	Location	Highlights / Things to Do	Fuel / Service	Campgrounds	Approx. Mileage from Start
1	Double J Campground (Chatham, IL)	RV park with full hookups, quiet and clean facilities	Nearby gas stations in Chatham and Springfield	Double J Campground & RV Park	0 mi
2	Springfield, IL	Visit Lincoln Home National Historic Site, Old State Capitol	Multiple gas stations and repair shops	KOA Springfield Route 66	10 mi
3	St. Louis, MO	Gateway Arch, Route 66 Start Marker	Major services available throughout the city	St. Louis West/Historic Route 66 KOA	95 mi
4	Route 66 State Park	Scenic walking trails, Route 66 Museum	Small fuel stops nearby in Eureka, MO	Jellystone Park near Eureka	135 mi

5	Cuba, MO	Murals along Route 66, Visit the Wagon Wheel Motel	Gas station at Route 66 Fudge Shop	Cuba KOA Journey	170 mi

Recommended RV Campground (St. Louis Area) Cahokia RV Parque

📍 *4060 Mississippi Ave, Cahokia, IL 62206* (10 minutes from downtown St. Louis)

Meramec Valley Campground and RV Park

📍 **3950 Highway ZZ, Cuba, MO 65453**

📞 Phone: +1 573-885-2541

Day 3 – From Cuba, MO to Tulsa, OK

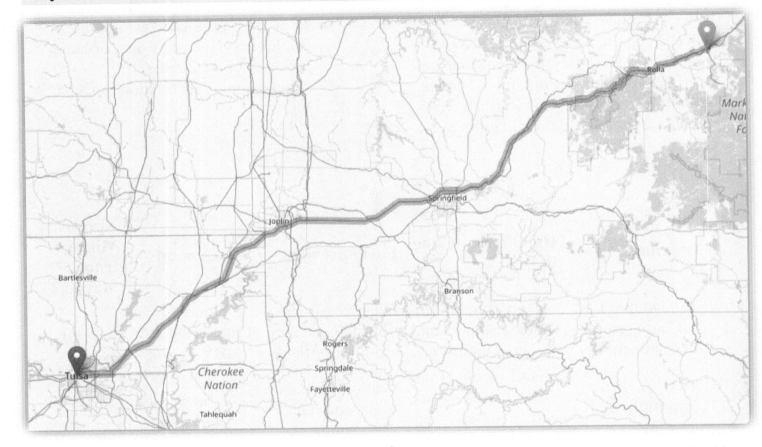

Directions: **Distance:** 312 miles
Estimated Time: 5 hours 34 minutes

1. Start on East Washington Boulevard (Historic Route 66) – 0.02 mi
2. Turn right onto North Franklin Street (MO 19) – 0.81 mi
3. Turn left onto the ramp toward I-44 West: Rolla – 0.19 mi
4. Merge left onto I-44 – 295.83 mi
5. At the fork, keep right to stay on I-44 – 4.97 mi
6. At the fork, keep right onto Martin Luther King, Jr. Memorial Expressway (I-244; US 412) – 8.70 mi

7. Take Exit 6C on the right toward 1st Street, Downtown – 0.25 mi
8. Continue on East 1st Street South – 0.68 mi
9. Turn right onto South Main Street – 0.07 mi
10. Arrive at your destination

Recommended Overnight Campgrounds

Option	Location	Distance from Start	Features
Coachlight RV Park	Carthage, MO	~240 mi	Full hookups, pull-through sites, near Route 66 Drive-In Theater
Tulsa RV Ranch	Tulsa, OK (Final Destination)	312 mi	Spacious lots, full hookups, laundry, Wi-Fi, propane refill, diner on-site
KOA Springfield/Rt 66	Springfield, MO	~160 mi	Good midway stop if you want to split the day; playground, pool, full amenities

Point of Interest	Location	Miles from Start	Notes
Uranus Fudge Factory	St. Robert, MO	~40 mi	Humorous Route 66 stop with gifts and fudge
Route 66 Museum	Lebanon, MO	~90 mi	Great for a break, free entry
Shepherd Hills Outlet	Lebanon, MO	~92 mi	Famous knife store, good stop
Gary's Gay Parita Station	Paris Springs	~140 mi	Restored Sinclair station with memorabilia
Jasper County Courthouse	Carthage, MO	~240 mi	Photo-worthy historic courthouse
Blue Whale of Catoosa	Catoosa, OK	~295 mi	Classic Route 66 roadside attraction

Location	Approx. Mileage	Notes
Lebanon, MO	~90 mi	Fuel, Walmart, cafes
Springfield, MO	~145 mi	Major services, attractions
Joplin, MO	~250 mi	Great RV services, fuel, historic markers
Tulsa, OK	Final	Plenty of refueling options before you head west again

From Murals to Memories

The stretch of Route 66 from Cuba, Missouri to Tulsa, Oklahoma offers a rich blend of small-town Americana, roadside nostalgia, and artistic charm. Starting in Cuba, known as the "Route 66 Mural City," travelers are immediately immersed in vibrant public art that captures moments of local and national history. As the road winds westward, the journey takes you through charming towns like Rolla and Lebanon, where vintage diners, gas stations, and classic motels keep the spirit of mid-century travel alive.

One highlight is Gary's Gay Parita in Paris Springs Junction, a lovingly recreated 1930s Sinclair gas station that feels like a living museum. As the road leads into the Ozarks and across the state line, the landscape shifts from rolling green hills to flatter, sunbaked stretches leading into Oklahoma.

Arriving in Tulsa, travelers are welcomed by a city that beautifully merges Route 66 history with modern culture. Tulsa's downtown offers restored Art Deco buildings, live music venues, and tributes to the Mother Road, making it a fitting destination to pause and reflect on the journey. This portion of the route is ideal for RV travelers looking to combine scenic views, cultural stops, and a relaxed pace that captures the true essence of Route 66.

Day 4 – From Tulsa, OK to Amarillo, TX

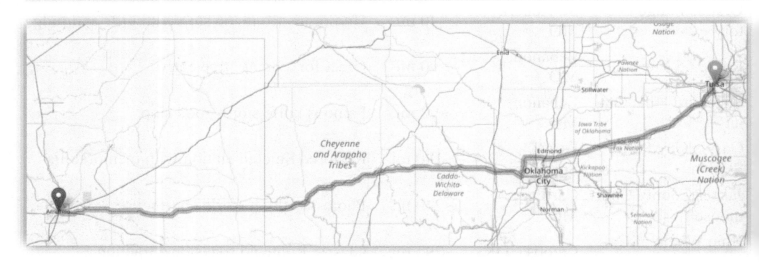

Directions: Distance: 365 miles – Time: 6 hours 18 minutes

1. Start on North Main Street in downtown Tulsa and drive 0.07 miles.
2. Turn right onto West 1st Street and continue for 0.37 miles.
3. Turn left onto the entrance ramp toward I-244 East / US-64 West / OK-51 West and continue for 0.04 miles.
4. Turn left onto South Heavy Traffic Way and drive 0.31 miles.
5. Turn right onto the ramp for I-244 West / US-75 South and continue for 0.25 miles.

14

6. Merge left onto I-244 West (Martin Luther King, Jr. Memorial Expressway) and drive for 2.3 miles.
7. Continue onto US-75 South (Okmulgee Expressway) for 1.55 miles.
8. Take the ramp on the right for I-44 West / OK-66 West toward Oklahoma City and continue for 0.68 miles.
9. Merge left onto I-44 West (Skelly Bypass / OK-66) and drive for 1.12 miles.
10. At the fork, keep left to stay on I-44 West / OK-66 for another 1.12 miles.
11. Continue on I-44 West (Turner Turnpike / Governor Roy J. Turner Turnpike) for 86.4 miles.
12. Merge onto I-44 West (John Kilpatrick Turnpike) near Oklahoma City and continue for 24.9 miles.
13. Take the ramp on the right toward I-40 West: Yukon, Amarillo and continue for 0.68 miles.
14. At the fork, turn left onto the connector road and continue for 0.12 miles.
15. Merge left onto I-40 West (Korean War Veterans Memorial Highway / US-270) and drive for 55.9 miles.
16. Continue on I-40 West (Senator Ed Berrong Memorial Highway) for 2.6 miles.
17. Continue on I-40 West (Korean War Veterans Memorial Highway) for 24.2 miles.
18. Continue on I-40 West (Great Western Cattle Trail segment) for 10.6 miles.
19. Continue on I-40 West (Korean War Veterans Memorial Highway) for 149.1 miles.
20. Take Exit 72B on the right toward Grand Street in Amarillo and drive for 0.19 miles.
21. Continue onto East Interstate Drive for 0.08 miles.
22. Turn right onto South Grand Street and continue for 0.05 miles.
23. Turn left onto East 16th Avenue and drive for 0.31 miles.
24. Continue on Tee Anchor Boulevard (Loop 395 / US-287 Historic Route) for 0.75 miles.
25. Continue on Southeast 10th Avenue (Loop 395 / US-287 Historic Route) for 1.18 miles.
26. Turn right onto South Lincoln Street and drive for 0.12 miles.
27. Turn left onto Southeast 8th Avenue and continue for 0.37 miles.
28. Turn right onto South Polk Street and drive 0.12 miles.
29. Arrive at your destination in **downtown Amarillo, TX**.

Scenic Drive Overview: Leaving Tulsa, you join the I-244 and then quickly merge onto the historic Skelly Bypass, which runs alongside the original Route 66 path. The landscape transitions from the green, wooded plains of Oklahoma to the wide-open sky and flat grasslands of the Texas Panhandle. This stretch of Route 66 is perfect for long-haul RV travel, with smooth roads and plenty of fuel stops. Along the Governor Roy Joseph Turner Turnpike, you'll pass through Oklahoma City before joining I-40 West toward Amarillo. This is where the journey really opens up—expansive skies, red earth, and straight-shot highways.

Points of Interest and Scenic Highlights

Location	Miles from Tulsa	Highlight
Route 66 Village, Tulsa, OK	5 mi	Historic oil derrick & restored train car – great photo stop
Arcadia Round Barn, Arcadia, OK	110 mi	Unique red barn built in 1898, quirky and iconic
Pops 66 Soda Ranch, Arcadia, OK	111 mi	66-foot soda bottle sculpture & 700+ sodas inside
Lucille's Historic Highway Gas Station, Hydro, OK	250 mi	A preserved 1920s gas station known as "Mother of the Mother Road"
Cadillac Ranch, Amarillo, TX	10 mi before destination	A must-see: 10 graffiti-covered Cadillacs buried nose-first in the dirt

Fuel & Supply Stops

Location	Services
Oklahoma City, OK	Major service area, groceries, RV-friendly gas stations
Elk City, OK	RV dump station, fast food, Walmart
Shamrock, TX	Tower Station and U-Drop Inn Café – vintage Route 66 gas station and diner

Recommended RV Campgrounds

Campground	Location	Amenities
Amarillo KOA Holiday	1100 Folsom Rd, Amarillo, TX 79108	Full hookups, Wi-Fi, pool, dog park, Route 66 mural
Overnite RV Park	10801 I-40 Frontage Rd, Amarillo, TX 79124	Affordable overnight, pull-throughs, clean showers
Oasis RV Resort	2715 Arnot Rd, Amarillo, TX 79124	Big-rig friendly, hot tub, playground, near Cadillac Ranch

Day 5 – From Amarillo, TX to Santa Rosa, NM

Directions: **Distance**: 171 miles
Time: 2 hours 56 minutes

1. Start on South Polk Street in Amarillo and drive south for 0.43 miles.
2. Turn left onto Southeast 12th Avenue and continue for 0.07 miles.
3. Turn right onto Canyon Expressway (US 287 South) and drive for 0.37 miles.
4. Bear slightly right to stay on US 287 South and continue for 0.09 miles.
5. At the fork, turn right onto the entrance ramp and continue for 0.25 miles.
6. Merge left onto I-40 West and drive for approximately 168 miles through the Texas panhandle and into eastern New Mexico.
7. Take the ramp on the right toward Santa Rosa and continue for 0.25 miles.
8. At the fork, turn right onto the connector road and drive for 0.06 miles.
9. Continue on Historic Route 66 (also signed as I-40 Business, US 54, and US 84) into Santa Rosa for 0.31 miles.
10. Turn left onto Lake Drive and continue for 0.43 miles.
11. Continue on La Pradira Avenue for 0.05 miles.
12. Arrive at your destination in **Santa Rosa, NM**.

Campground Recommendation

Santa Rosa Campground & RV Park
2136 Historic Route 66, Santa Rosa, NM 88435 📞 (575) 472-3126

🔧 Fuel & Services

- **Gas & Diesel Stations:Love's Travel Stop** in Vega, TX (~45 mi), **Pilot Travel Center** in Tucumcari, NM (~130 mi)
- **Groceries & Supplies**:
  - **Lowe's Market** in Tucumcari
  - **Family Dollar** and **Dollar General** in Santa Rosa

Points of Interest and Scenic Highlights:

Location	Mile Marker (from Amarillo)	What to See & Do
Cadillac Ranch (TX)	10 mi	Iconic public art installation with buried Cadillacs. Bring spray paint!
Adrian, TX (Midpoint)	50 mi	Midpoint Café – the halfway point of Route 66! Classic diner with vintage charm.
Tucumcari, NM	130 mi	Known for vibrant murals, vintage motels, and the iconic Blue Swallow Motel. Don't miss the Route 66 Museum.
Santa Rosa, NM	171 mi	Home to the Blue Hole, a deep natural spring perfect for swimming, and the Route 66 Auto Museum with classic cars and memorabilia.

Day 6 – From Santa Rosa, NM to Gallup, NM

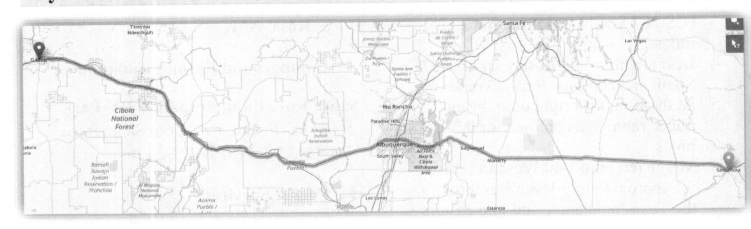

Directions: **Distance**: 254 miles
Time: 4 hours 23 minutes

1. Start on La Pradira Avenue – 0.12 mi
2. Turn right onto South 3rd Street (NM 91) – 0.31 mi
3. At the end of the road, turn left onto Historic Route 66 (I-40 BUS; US 54; US 84) – 1.18 mi
4. Turn right onto the ramp toward I-40 BUS; US 84 – 249.80 mi
5. Take the ramp on the right toward Miyamura Drive, Montoya Boulevard – 0.31 mi
6. Turn right onto Ford Drive (NM 609) – 0.09 mi
7. Turn left onto Joseph M Montoya Boulevard (NM 609) – 0.93 mi
8. Continue on West Maloney Avenue (NM 609) – 0.18 mi
9. Turn left onto South 3rd Street (NM 610) – 0.25 mi

10. Turn left onto West Historic Highway 66 (I-40 BUS; NM 118; US 66 Hist) – 0.04 mi

11. Arrive at your destination

Mile Marker (from Santa Rosa)	Attraction/Stop	Details
0 mi	Route 66 Auto Museum – Santa Rosa	Start your day with classic cars and memorabilia.
46 mi	Tucumcari, NM	Murals, the Blue Swallow Motel, and a vibrant downtown.
130 mi	Route 66 Monument – Albuquerque (Detour Option)	Optional scenic detour to visit Old Town and the monument.
160–200 mi	Scenic Views of Red Mesas and Plateaus	Between Grants and Gallup, watch for red rock formations and mesas.
240 mi	Red Rock Park – Gallup	Great for hiking or quick panoramic views of the area.
254 mi	Historic Gallup Downtown	Browse Native American crafts, dine, or visit the historic El Rancho Hotel.

Recommended Campground for Overnight Stay

USA RV Park – Gallup, NM. Address: 2925 W Historic Hwy 66, Gallup, NM 87301

- **Phone**: +1 505-863-5021
- **Website**: www.usarvpark.com

Day 7 – From Gallup, NM to Williams, AZ

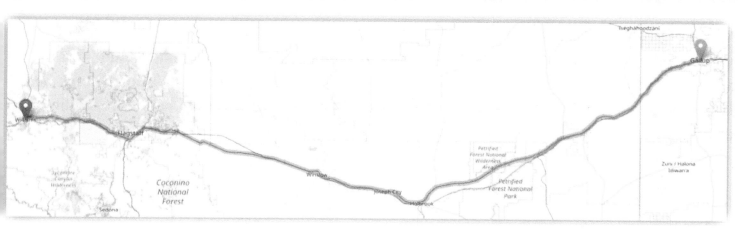

Directions: Distance: 219 miles – **Estimated Time**: 3 hours 44 minutes

1. Start on West Historic Highway 66 (I-40 BUS; NM 118; Historic US 66) – 0.05 mi
2. Turn left onto South 2nd Street (NM 610) – 0.25 mi
3. Turn left onto West Maloney Avenue (NM 609) – 0.93 mi
4. Turn left onto US 491 – 0.07 mi
5. Take the ramp on the right toward I-40 West – 0.31 mi
6. Merge left onto I-40 – 216 mi
7. Take the ramp on the right toward Williams, Grand Canyon – 0.37 mi
8. Turn left onto North Grand Canyon Boulevard – 0.68 mi
9. Arrive at your destination

Location	Type	Details	Distance from Gallup
Grand Canyon Railway RV Park	RV Campground	Full hookups, laundry, Wi-Fi, walkable to Williams downtown.	Approx. 345 km / 214 mi
Canyon Motel & RV Park	RV Campground	Vintage railcars, pine trees, quiet sites with full hookups.	Approx. 347 km / 215 mi
Red Rock Park	Scenic Spot / Hike	Sandstone formations, good for photos and short hikes.	Approx. 10 km / 6 mi
Continental Divide Marker	Photo / Landmark Stop	Geographic marker, quick roadside photo opportunity.	Approx. 48 km / 30 mi
Winslow	AZ	Historic Town / Food Stop	Historic Route 66 site with photo ops and local diners.
Painted Desert / Petrified Forest National Park	National Park / Detour	Colorful badlands and fossilized wood, 1-2 hr scenic detour.	Approx. 160 km / 99 mi (via detour)

What to See Along the Way: Along the drive from Gallup to Williams, highlights include the vibrant red cliffs of **Red Rock Park**, the symbolic **Continental Divide marker**, and—if time allows—a detour to the breathtaking **Painted Desert and Petrified Forest National Park** near Holbrook. Don't miss a fun photo stop in **Winslow, Arizona**, home of the famous "Standin' on the Corner" mural inspired by the Eagles' song.

Day 8 – From Williams, AZ to Las Vegas

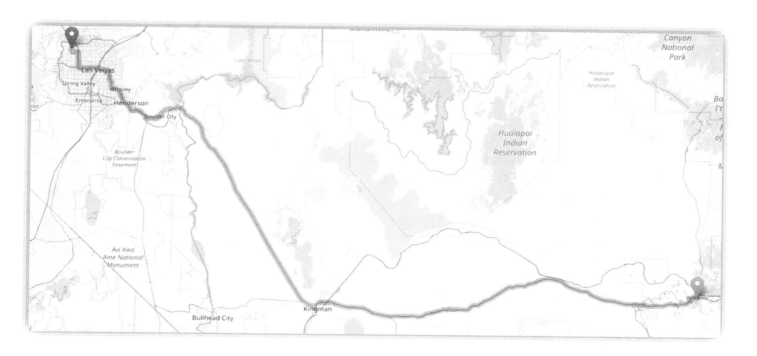

Directions: **Distance: 230 miles – Time: 4:17**

1. Start on North Grand Canyon Boulevard in Williams and drive north for 0.68 miles.
2. Turn left onto the entrance ramp to I-40 West and continue for 0.43 miles.
3. Merge left onto I-40 West (Purple Heart Trail) and drive for approximately 113 miles.
4. Take the ramp on the right toward US-93 North (exit for Kingman and Hoover Dam) and continue for 0.31 miles.
5. At the fork, turn right onto US-93 North and continue for 0.05 miles.
6. Merge left onto Beale Street (which carries US-93) and drive through Kingman for 28 miles.
7. Continue on US-93 North through the scenic desert highway for 30 miles.
8. Continue again on US-93 North as you approach the Hoover Dam Bypass for 13.6 miles.
9. Take exit 2 on the right toward US-93 Business North / NV-172 East: Boulder City, Hoover Dam, Lake Mead and drive for 0.12 miles.
10. At the fork, turn right onto US-93 Business and continue for 0.37 miles.
11. Continue on Boulder City Parkway (US-93 Business) for 9.3 miles through Boulder City.
12. Merge onto I-11 North (Purple Heart Highway / US-93 / US-95) and drive for 31 miles into the Las Vegas area.
13. Take exit 85 on the right toward Craig Road and drive for 0.25 miles.
14. At the fork, turn left onto the connector road for 0.05 miles.
15. Turn left onto West Craig Road (NV-573) and continue for 1.86 miles.

16. Turn right onto North Durango Drive and drive for 0.87 miles.

17. Arrive at your destination in Las Vegas, NV.

Road Notes for the RV Traveler: US 93 North between Kingman and Boulder City offers *breathtaking desert landscapes*, especially around **Black Mountains** and **Lake Mead National Recreation Area**.

- **Beale Street** in Kingman is rich with Route 66 charm—great for a coffee or stroll.
- **Hoover Dam Bypass Bridge** is a brief detour but offers one of the most iconic views in the American Southwest.
- **Traffic Alert:** Approaching Las Vegas from Boulder City can see congestion, especially during weekends—plan accordingly.

Scenic Highlights and Roadside Attractions:

Mile Marker (from Williams, AZ)	Location	What to See or Do
0 mi	Williams, AZ	Historic downtown, Grand Canyon Railway, Route 66 diners. A great photo stop before departure.
~60 mi	Ash Fork, AZ	Known as the "Flagstone Capital of the World," look for small Route 66 museums and signage.
~90 mi	Seligman, AZ (Optional Detour)	Iconic Route 66 town—stop at Delgadillo's Snow Cap Drive-In, quirky gift shops, and murals.
~170 mi	Kingman, AZ	Visit the Route 66 Museum, the Powerhouse Visitor Center, and enjoy lunch at Mr. D'z Route 66 Diner.
~205 mi	Hoover Dam (Short Detour via Boulder City)	Scenic photo opportunity, engineering marvel, and visitor center tours available.
~230 mi	Las Vegas, NV	Entertainment capital with RV-friendly campgrounds, shopping, dining, and bright lights.

Recommended RV Campground for the Night

Las Vegas KOA at Sam's Town

Address: 5225 Boulder Hwy, Las Vegas, NV 89122 - **Website:** koa.com/campgrounds/las-vegas
Phone: +1 702-454-8055

Oasis Las Vegas RV Resort

Address: 2711 W Windmill Ln, Las Vegas, NV 89123 - **Website:** oasislasvegasrvresort.com
Phone: +1 702-260-2020

Fuel & Supplies Stops (Recommended)

- **Love's Travel Stop – Kingman, AZ** (Easy access for large RVs)
- **Chevron – Boulder City, NV** (near Hoover Dam detour)
- **Walmart Supercenter – Las Vegas, NV** (Stock up before continuing west)

Day 9 – From Las Vegas to Santa Monica

Directions: Distance: 297 miles — **Time:** 5 hours and 32 minutes

1. Start on North Durango Drive in Las Vegas and drive for 0.87 miles
2. Turn left onto West Craig Road and continue for 1.74 miles
3. Turn right onto the ramp toward US-95 South and continue for 0.37 miles
4. Merge left onto I-95 South (Purple Heart Highway / I-11) and drive for 8.08 miles
5. Take exit 76B-C on the right toward I-15 South: Los Angeles / Martin L. King Boulevard and continue for 0.50 miles
6. At the fork, turn left onto the connector road and continue for 0.99 miles
7. At the next fork, turn right and continue for 0.68 miles
8. At the next fork, turn left and continue for 0.62 miles
9. Merge left onto I-15 South (Las Vegas Freeway) and continue for 41.00 miles
10. Continue on I-15 South (Mojave Freeway) for 5.59 miles
11. At the fork, stay left to continue on I-15 South (Mojave Freeway) for 150.37 miles
12. Continue on I-15 South (Barstow and Mojave Freeway / Heavy Traffic Route) for 1.55 miles
13. Continue on I-15 South (Mojave Freeway) for 11.18 miles
14. Continue again on I-15 South (Barstow and Mojave Freeway) for 0.62 miles
15. At the fork, turn left onto I-15 South (Ontario Freeway) and drive 9.32 miles
16. Continue on I-15 South (CHP Officer John Bailey Memorial Freeway) for 0.75 miles
17. Continue on I-15 South (Ontario Freeway) for 4.97 miles

18. Take exit 109A on the right toward I-10 West: Los Angeles and continue for 0.50 miles
19. Merge left onto I-10 West (San Bernardino Freeway) and drive 1.49 miles
20. Take the ramp on the left and continue for 0.03 miles
21. Merge left onto I-10 Express Lanes and continue for 7.45 miles
22. Merge right back onto I-10 West (San Bernardino Freeway) and continue for 18.02 miles
23. Take exit 31A on the right toward I-605 South: San Gabriel River Freeway and continue for 0.19 miles
24. At the fork, turn left onto the connector road and drive 0.43 miles
25. Merge left onto I-605 South (San Gabriel River Freeway) and continue for 2.24 miles
26. Take exit 19 toward CA-60 East / CA-60 West: Pomona Freeway and continue for 0.19 miles
27. At the fork, turn right onto the connector road and continue for 0.25 miles

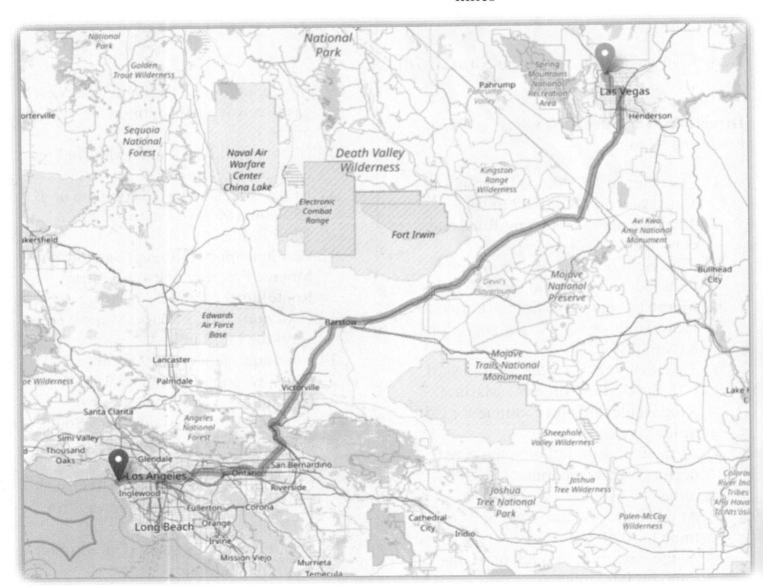

28. Merge left onto CA-60 West (Pomona Freeway) and drive for 10.56 miles
29. Continue on CA-60 West (Pomona Freeway) for 1.24 miles
30. Merge right onto I-10 West (Santa Monica Freeway) and drive for 2.98 miles
31. At the fork, stay right to continue on I-10 West (Santa Monica Freeway) for 12.43 miles
32. Take exit 1B on the right toward CA-1 South: Lincoln Boulevard and continue for 0.19 miles
33. Continue onto Olympic Boulevard for 0.09 miles
34. Turn right onto Lincoln Boulevard and drive 0.43 miles
35. Arrive at your destination in **Santa Monica, CA**

Overnight Stay Recommendation

Campground Name	Location	Amenities	Distance to Santa Monica Pier
Dockweiler RV Park	12001 Vista Del Mar, Playa Del Rey, CA 90293	Full hookups, beachfront views, dump station, showers, laundry, picnic tables	~7 miles (~15 minutes)
Malibu Beach RV Park	25801 Pacific Coast Hwy, Malibu, CA 90265	Ocean views, full hookups, Wi-Fi, general store, pet-friendly	~20 miles (~35 minutes)

Location	Mileage from Start	What to See / Do
Barstow, CA	~160 mi	Route 66 Mother Road Museum, desert scenery, outlet shopping
Victorville, CA	~195 mi	California Route 66 Museum, old-town architecture
Cajon Pass	~215 mi	Dramatic descent from desert into SoCal valleys, panoramic highway views
San Bernardino	~235 mi	Visit the site of the first McDonald's (now a museum), vibrant Latino culture
Downtown LA	~270 mi	Optional detour: Olvera Street, Union Station, Griffith Park
Santa Monica Pier	297 mi	The official end of Route 66 — take a picture with the historic "End of the Trail" sign

PACIFIC COAST HIGHWAY (CALIFORNIA STATE ROUTE 1)

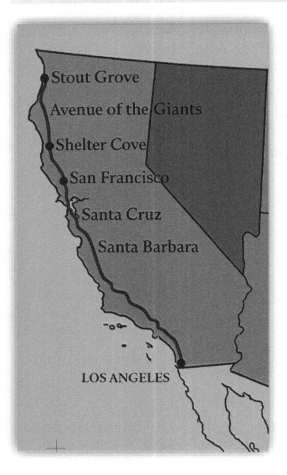

The **Pacific Coast Highway (PCH)**—officially known as **California State Route 1**—is one of the most iconic and scenic drives in the United States, and perhaps the world. **Why It's Famous:** Route 1 is renowned for being **one of the most beautiful coastal highways in the world**. With the road hugging dramatic ocean cliffs and weaving through charming towns, travelers are treated to stunning panoramic views, pristine beaches, and historic landmarks throughout the drive.

Perfect for RV Travelers: The Pacific Coast Highway is a **dream route for RV adventures**. There are numerous coastal campgrounds and RV parks with full hookups, scenic pull-through sites, and modern amenities. You'll find fuel stations, grocery stores, and RV services in all major towns. Many viewpoints along the coast have designated pullouts large enough for motorhomes.

General Overview:

Starting Point: Dana Point, Orange County, CA
Ending Point: Leggett, Mendocino County, CA
Total Length: Approx. **650 miles (1,050 km)**
Scenery: Coastal cliffs, sandy beaches, redwood forests, seaside towns

Must-See Stops Along the Route:

Location	Main Attraction
Santa Monica	Iconic pier, symbolic end of Route 66
Malibu	Surfer beaches, celebrity homes, Zuma Beach
Santa Barbara	Spanish colonial architecture, wine tasting
San Luis Obispo	Mission San Luis Obispo, quirky Madonna Inn
Big Sur	Bixby Creek Bridge, McWay Falls, rugged cliffs
Monterey & Carmel	Monterey Bay Aquarium, 17-Mile Drive, art galleries
Santa Cruz	Classic boardwalk, surf culture, eclectic vibe
San Francisco	Golden Gate Bridge, Alcatraz, historic Presidio
Mendocino & Beyond	Tranquil coastal towns, redwood forests

Day 1 – From Leggett, CA to Point Arena, CA

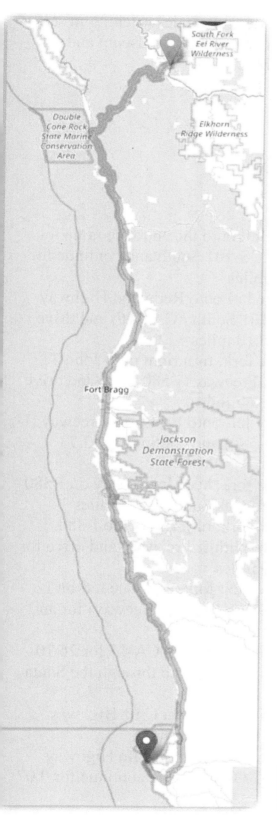

Directions: **Distance:** 89 miles
Time: 2 hours 27 minutes

1.   Start on Drive-Thru Tree Road (CA 271) – 0.19 mi
2.   At the end of the road, turn left onto California State Route 1 (CA 1) – 25.48 mi
3.   Continue on Shoreline Highway (CA 1) – 15.53 mi
4.   Continue on North Main Street (CA 1) – 3.73 mi
5.   Continue on Shoreline Highway (CA 1) – 0.50 mi
6.   At the roundabout, take the 2nd exit onto Shoreline Highway (CA 1) – 0.03 mi
7.   Exit the roundabout onto Shoreline Highway (CA 1) – 18.02 mi
8.   Turn right onto Shoreline Highway (CA 1) – 22.37 mi
9.   Turn sharp right onto Lighthouse Road – 2.61 mi
10.   Arrive at your destination

Things to Do Along the Route

Stop	Distance from Start	Description
Drive-Thru Tree Park	0 mi	Begin your journey by driving through a giant redwood—a true California roadside classic.
Mendocino Coast Botanical Gardens (Optional stop near Fort Bragg)	~30 mi	A peaceful walk among native plants and coastal cliffs. RV parking available.
Point Arena-Stornetta Public Lands	~85 mi	Scenic trails with views of blowholes, sea arches, and dramatic cliffs. Ideal for photos and sunset views.

Recommended RV Campground

Point Arena Lighthouse Keepers RV Campground
- 45500 Lighthouse Road, Point Arena, CA 95468
- pointarenalighthouse.com
- (707) 882-2809

Point Arena Lighthouse	89 mi	End of Day 1: Historic lighthouse with panoramic views of the Pacific and whale-watching in season. Includes a museum and gift shop.

Day 2 – From Point Arena, CA to Santa Cruz

Directions: **Distance: 209 miles | Time: 4:53**

1. Start on Lighthouse Road heading east and drive for 2.61 miles
2. Turn right onto Shoreline Highway (CA-1 South) and continue for 1.24 miles
3. Continue on School Street (still CA-1) for 0.50 miles
4. Turn right onto Main Street (CA-1) and drive for 0.56 miles
5. Continue on Shoreline Highway (CA-1) for 14.91 miles through the rugged Mendocino Coast
6. Continue on Coast Highway (CA-1) for 46.60 miles, passing through small towns like Jenner and Bodega Bay
7. Continue on Bay Highway (CA-1) for 5.59 miles
8. Continue on Valley Ford Cutoff (CA-1) for 2.92 miles
9. Continue on Valley Ford Road (CA-1) for 5.59 miles
10. Turn left onto Roblar Road and drive inland for 6.21 miles
11. At the end of Roblar Road, turn right onto Stony Point Road and continue for 3.11 miles
12. Turn left onto the entrance ramp toward US-101 South and continue for 0.12 miles
13. Merge left onto Redwood Highway (US-101 South / CA-116) and drive for 26.10 miles
14. At the fork, turn right onto John T. Knox Freeway (I-580 East) and drive for 13.67 miles
15. Merge left onto Eastshore Freeway (I-80 / I-580) and continue for 3.73 miles
16. At the fork, keep left to stay on I-580 toward Oakland for 0.25 miles
17. At the fork, turn right onto I-880 South (Nimitz Freeway) and drive for 14.29 miles
18. At the next fork, continue left on I-880 South (Nimitz Freeway) for another 31.69 miles
19. Continue south on CA-17 for 26.10 miles as you climb through the Santa Cruz Mountains
20. Continue on Santa Cruz Highway (CA-17) for 0.25 miles
21. Merge left onto Cabrillo Highway (CA-1 / CA-17) and continue for 0.07 miles

22. At the fork, turn right to stay on Cabrillo Highway (CA-1) for 1.12 miles
23. Continue on Chestnut Street Extension for 0.31 miles
24. Turn right onto Walnut Avenue and continue for 0.19 miles
25. Turn left onto California Street and drive for 0.62 miles

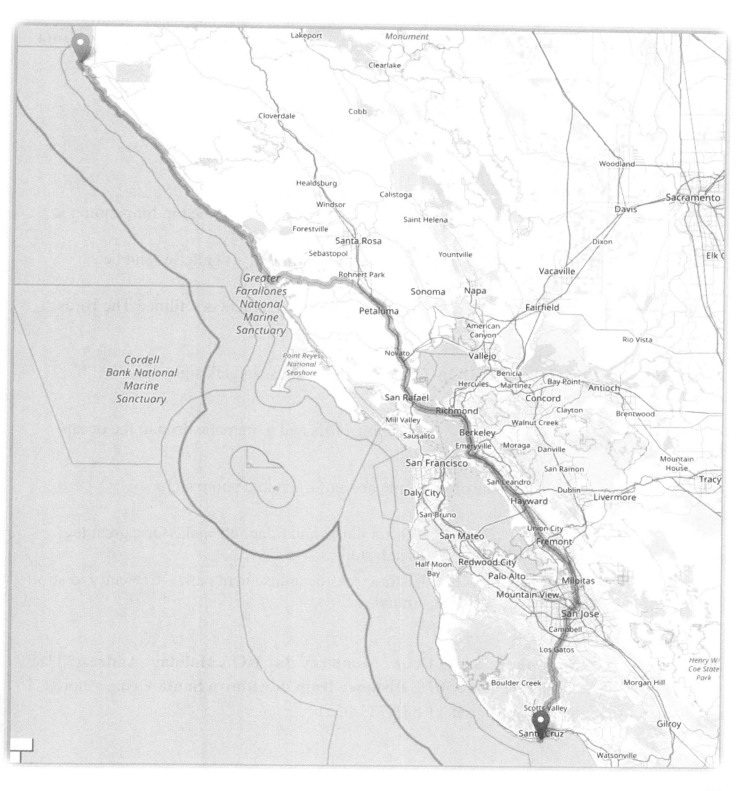

26. At the end of California Street, turn left onto Bay Street and drive for 0.19 miles
27. Turn right onto Columbia Street for 0.01 miles
28. Slight left to stay on Columbia Street for 0.56 miles
29. At the end of the road, turn right onto Pelton Avenue for 0.01 miles
30. Turn left onto Columbia Street again and continue for 0.06 miles
31. Turn left onto the unnamed driveway or private road for 0.06 miles
32. Arrive at your destination in **Santa Cruz, CA**

Mile Marker (from Point Arena Lighthouse)	Location/Highlight	Notes
0 mi	Point Arena Lighthouse	Start the day with a climb to the top for panoramic ocean views.
~25 mi	Gualala	Small coastal town with art galleries and beach access.
~75 mi	Bodega Bay	Classic seafood stop; Hitchcock filmed The Birds here.
~130 mi	Point Reyes National Seashore (Optional detour)	Offers trails, beaches, and elk sightings.
~170 mi	Muir Beach Overlook	Sweeping cliffs and a dramatic drop to the ocean.
~200 mi	Golden Gate Bridge (crossed via nearby detour)	Iconic and unforgettable photo stop.
~230 mi	Half Moon Bay	Coastal bluffs and tidepools make for a great leg-stretch stop.
~290 mi	Santa Cruz Beach Boardwalk	Historic seaside amusement park—free entry to stroll around.

Recommended Campground: Santa Cruz / Monterey Bay KOA Holiday: **Address:** 1186 San Andreas Rd, Watsonville, CA 95076. **Distance from downtown Santa Cruz:** Approx. 15 miles south (~30 min drive). **Phone:** +1 831-722-0551

Day 3 – From Santa Cruz to Monterey to San Simeon

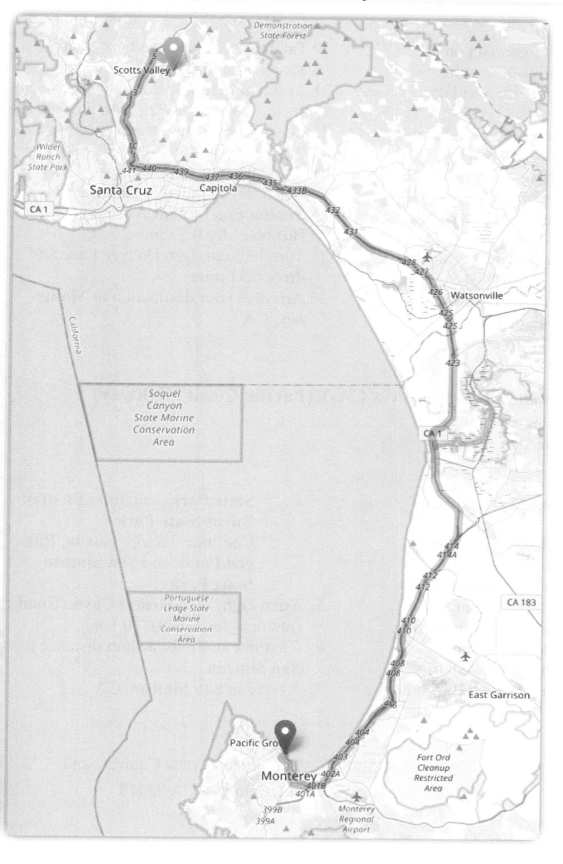

Directions: **Distance:** 45 miles
Time: 57 minutes

1. Start on Columbia Street and drive 0.06 miles
2. Turn right onto Pelton Avenue and drive 0.01 miles
3. Turn left onto Columbia Street and continue for 0.25 miles
4. Turn right onto Delaware Avenue and continue for 0.25 miles
5. Continue on Laguna Street for 0.12 miles
6. At the end of the road, turn right onto Bay Street and drive 0.19 miles
7. Turn left onto West Cliff Drive and continue for 0.07 miles
8. Continue on Beach Street for 0.08 miles
9. At the roundabout, take the 3rd exit onto Pacific Avenue and continue for 0.04 miles
10. Exit the roundabout to stay on Pacific Avenue and drive 0.19 miles

11. At the next roundabout, take the 1st exit to continue on Pacific Avenue for 0.006 miles
12. Exit the roundabout to remain on Pacific Avenue and drive 0.12 miles
13. Turn right onto Front Street and drive 0.19 miles
14. Turn right onto Laurel Street and continue for 0.10 miles
15. Slight left onto Broadway and continue for 0.31 miles
16. Turn left onto Ocean Street and drive for 0.09 miles
17. Turn right onto Soquel Avenue and drive 0.81 miles
18. Turn left onto Morrissey Boulevard and continue for 0.43 miles
19. Turn right onto the ramp to merge onto CA-1 South and continue for 39 miles
20. Take exit 401A on the right toward Monterey and drive 0.31 miles
21. At the fork, turn left onto the connector road and drive 0.04 miles
22. Continue on Fremont Street (CA-1 Business) for 0.56 miles
23. Turn left onto Abrego Street (CA-1 Business) and drive 0.19 miles
24. Continue on Munras Avenue (CA-1 Business) for 0.37 miles
25. Turn left onto Don Dahvee Lane and drive 0.31 miles
26. Arrive at your destination in **Monterey, CA**

Directions: Monterey to San Simeon via CA-1 (Pacific Coast Highway)

Distance: Approx. 94 miles
Estimated Driving Time: 2 hours 30 minutes (without stops)

1. **Start** on **Don Dahvee Lane** in Monterey
2. **Turn right** onto **Munras Avenue (CA 1 Business South)** – 0.4 mi
3. **Merge right** onto the **ramp for CA-1 South** toward **Carmel** – 0.2 mi
4. **Merge** onto **Cabrillo Highway (CA 1 South)** – continue for ~90 miles
    o Pass through **Carmel-by-the-Sea, Big Sur, Pfeiffer Big Sur State Park**, and **Julia Pfeiffer Burns State Park**
    o Continue through **Gorda, Ragged Point**, and **San Simeon State Park**
5. **Turn right** onto **Hearst Castle Road** (optional for a visit) – 0.1 mi
6. Continue south for a short distance to **San Simeon**
7. **Arrive** in **San Simeon**, CA

Recommended RV Campground (Night in San Simeon): San Simeon Creek Campground – Hearst San Simeon State Park ● 500 San Simeon Creek Rd, Cambria, CA 93428

Location	Mile Marker from Santa Cruz	What to See & Do
Santa Cruz		Visit the Boardwalk, Surfing Museum, and West Cliff Drive
Monterey	45 mi	Explore Cannery Row, the Monterey Bay Aquarium, and Fisherman's Wharf
17-Mile Drive (optional)	52 mi	Detour through Pebble Beach with stunning coastal views
Big Sur	75–115 mi	Bixby Creek Bridge, Pfeiffer Beach, McWay Falls at Julia Pfeiffer Burns State Park
Ragged Point	140 mi	Epic cliff views and a great rest stop with food & fuel
Elephant Seal Vista Point	152 mi	Watch elephant seals lounging and battling on the beach
San Simeon	160 mi	Tour Hearst Castle and stroll the serene beaches

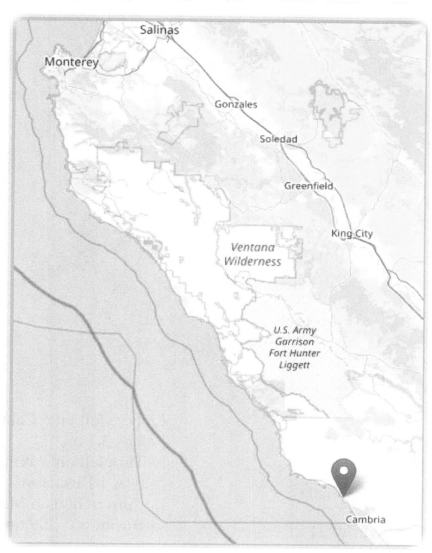

Day 4 – From San Simeon to Santa Barbara

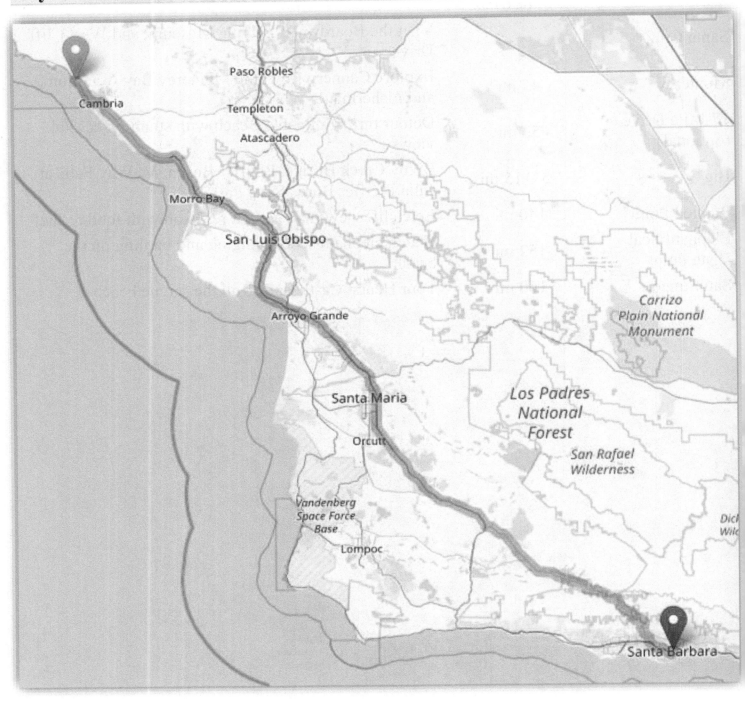

Directions: **Distance**: 132 miles
Estimated Time: 2 hours 53 minutes

1. Start on Castillo Drive – 0.31 mi

2. Turn left onto Cabrillo Highway (CA 1) – 3.7 mi
3. Turn left onto Windsor Boulevard (CA 1 Business) – 0.02 mi
4. Turn right onto Main Street (CA 1 Business) – 2.9 mi

5. Turn left onto Cabrillo Highway (CA 1) – 29.8 mi
6. Continue on North Santa Rosa Street (CA 1) – 1.7 mi
7. Turn right onto Olive Street (CA 1) – 0.12 mi
8. Turn right onto the ramp – 0.06 mi
9. Merge left onto Cabrillo Highway (US 101; CA 1) – 11.8 mi
10. Continue on El Camino Real (US 101) – 44.7 mi
11. Take the ramp on the right toward CA 154: Los Olivos, Lake Cachuma – 0.25 mi
12. Turn left onto Chumash Highway (CA 154) – 8.7 mi
13. At the roundabout, take the 2nd exit onto Chumash Highway (CA 154) – 0.02 mi
14. Exit the roundabout onto Chumash Highway (CA 154) – 24.2 mi
15. Turn left onto the ramp toward US 101 South – 0.25 mi
16. Merge left onto El Camino Real (US 101) – 3.1 mi
17. Take exit 98A on the right toward Carrillo Street, Downtown – 0.25 mi
18. Turn left onto West Carrillo Street – 0.37 mi
19. Turn left onto Chapala Street – 0.1 mi
20. Turn right onto West Figueroa Street – 0.18 mi
21. Turn right onto Anacapa Street – 0.05 mi
22. Turn right onto unnamed road – 0.08 mi
23. Arrive at your destination

Recommended Campground for Overnight Stay: Santa Barbara Sunrise RV Park: *516 S Salinas St, Santa Barbara, CA 93103* 📞 *(805) 966-9954*

🛢 Location	Services	Exit/Access
Paso Robles	Gas, Propane, Grocery	Easily accessible from US-101
San Luis Obispo	RV Dump Station, Super-markets	Exit Marsh St.
Pismo Beach Shell Station	Large bay, propane fill	Off CA-1 near Price St.
Santa Maria	RV repair shops, Walmart	Accessible from US-101

Location	Estimated Time	Notes
Moonstone Beach (Cambria)	15 min	Scenic boardwalk with ocean views; great for stretching your legs.
Morro Rock (Morro Bay)	30 min	A volcanic plug rising from the ocean—perfect photo op and picnic stop.

Pismo Beach	45–60 min	Explore sand dunes, grab a seafood lunch, or walk the pier.
Gaviota Coastline	Drive-through	Coastal bluffs, wildflowers, and surf spots along a less-developed stretch.
Santa Barbara Mission	Optional Detour	Visit the historic "Queen of the Missions" and its rose gardens.

Scenic Alert:

This drive features **coastal cliffs**, **rolling hills**, and **oceanfront farmland**. Keep your eyes open near:

- **Ragged Point**: One of the most dramatic ocean overlooks on the Central Coast
- **Avila Beach**: Secluded cove with calm waters and scenic boardwalk
- **Gaviota Pass**: Where the highway cuts through the coastal mountains

Day 5 – From Santa Barbara to Dana Point

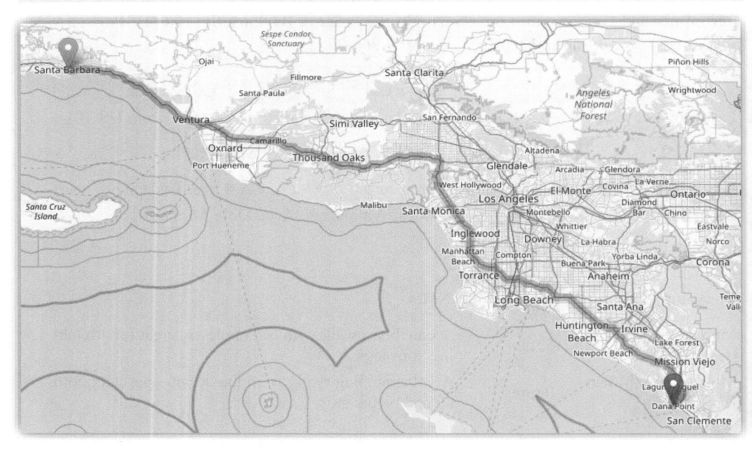

Directions: Distance: 155 miles | Time: 3:05

1. Start from East Ortega Street near the downtown area and drive 0.04 miles
2. Turn right onto Laguna Street and continue for 0.05 miles
3. At the end of the road, turn right onto Anacapa Street and drive 0.04 miles
4. Turn left onto East Carrillo Street and continue for 0.19 miles
5. Turn right onto Garden Street and drive 0.68 miles
6. Turn left onto the on-ramp for US-101 South and continue for 0.19 miles
7. Merge left onto US-101 South (El Camino Real) and drive for 3.7 miles
8. Continue on US-101 Freeway for 6.8 miles
9. Continue on Ventura Freeway (US-101) for 18.6 miles
10. Keep left to stay on Ventura Freeway (US-101 South) and continue for 47.8 miles
11. Take the ramp on the right toward I-405 North / I-405 South: Sacramento / Santa Monica and continue for 0.12 miles
12. At the fork, turn right onto South Sepulveda Boulevard and drive 0.31 miles
13. At the next fork, turn left onto the entrance ramp to I-405 and drive 0.11 miles
14. Merge left onto I-405 South (San Diego Freeway) and drive 39.8 miles
15. Keep right to stay on I-405 South and continue for 2.2 miles
16. Keep left on I-405 South (San Diego Freeway) and continue for 10.6 miles
17. At the fork, take the right exit onto CA-73 South (Corona Del Mar Freeway) and continue for 3.7 miles
18. Continue on CA-73 South (San Joaquin Hills Transportation Corridor — toll road) for 10.6 miles
19. Take Exit 3 on the right toward La Paz Road / Moulton Parkway and drive for 0.08 miles
20. At the fork, turn left onto La Paz Road and continue for 0.5 miles
21. At the fork, turn right onto Alicia Parkway and continue for 0.31 miles
22. Turn right onto Moulton Parkway and drive for 2.0 miles
23. Continue onto Golden Lantern Street and drive 5.6 miles
24. Arrive at your destination in **Dana Point, CA**

Recommended Campground for Overnight Stay: Doheny State Beach Campground:
25300 Dana Point Harbor Dr, Dana Point, CA 92629 +1 949-496-6172

Stop	Location	Description	Mile Marker (from SB)
Carpinteria State Beach	Carpinteria, CA	Gentle beach, tidepools, great for a short coffee break	~12 mi

Ventura Pier	Ventura, CA	Vintage pier with eateries and ocean views	~30 mi
Malibu	Malibu, CA	Scenic cliffs, iconic beaches (Zuma, El Matador), surfer culture	~85 mi
Santa Monica Pier	Santa Monica, CA	End of Route 66 marker, amusement park, and shops	~96 mi
Laguna Beach Lookouts	Laguna Beach, CA	Coastal cliffs and art town vibes; great photo stops	~140 mi

Dana Point: The Gateway to the Pacific

Nestled between the golden beaches of **Laguna Beach** and the vibrant harbor town of **San Clemente**, **Dana Point** is often referred to as the "Whale Capital of the West." Its dramatic cliffs, calm harbor, and easygoing surf culture make it a peaceful, yet captivating end to a road trip along California's scenic coastline.

Historically, Dana Point is named after **Richard Henry Dana Jr.**, a Harvard-educated sailor who described the area in his 1840 memoir *Two Years Before the Mast*. He called the nearby headland "the only romantic spot on the coast," and to this day, the name fits.

The town grew around **Dana Point Harbor**, a bustling marina built in the 1970s that today hosts fishing charters, whale watching tours, and laid-back waterfront restaurants. On a good day, dolphins leap in the surf, and gray whales migrate just beyond the horizon.

What to Do in Dana Point:

- **Visit the Ocean Institute**: An interactive marine science center located right on the water.
- **Hike the Dana Point Headlands Conservation Area**: Short trails with sweeping ocean views and native plants.
- **Stroll or picnic at Doheny State Beach**: Perfect for RV campers, surfers, and sunset lovers alike.
- **Take a whale-watching tour**: Seasonal migrations offer incredible views of gray and blue whales.

Why It Belongs in Your RV Atlas: Dana Point offers everything an RVer needs to unwind—full-service campgrounds like **Doheny State Beach**, beachside parking, fresh seafood, and a sense of finality only the ocean can provide. It's the natural bookend to an epic journey down the Pacific Coast—where the road meets the sea and reflections become memories.

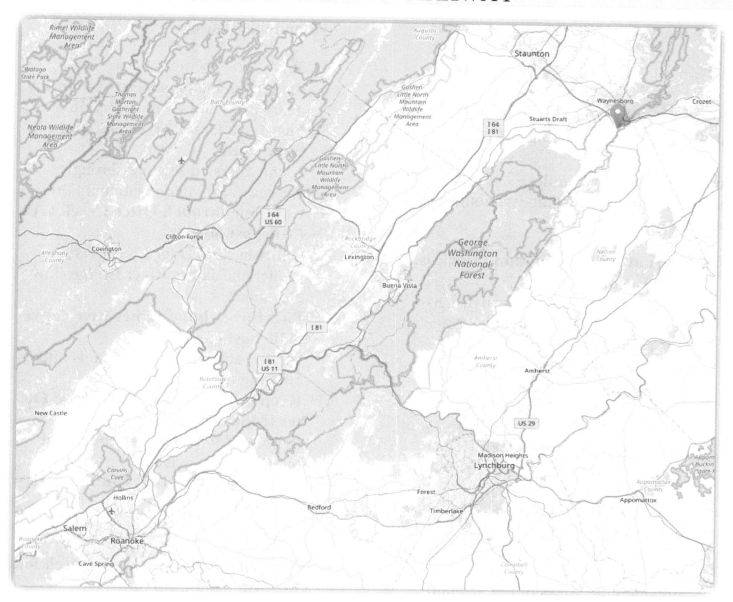

Introduction to the Blue Ridge Parkway: The **Blue Ridge Parkway** is more than just a road — it's a journey through time, nature, and the soul of the American South. Stretching **469 miles** through the Appalachian Highlands from **Afton, Virginia**, to **Cherokee, North Carolina**, this scenic byway links **Shenandoah National Park** in the north with the **Great Smoky Mountains National Park** in the south. Built during the Great Depression as part of President Roosevelt's New Deal, the Parkway was designed not only to connect parks, but to preserve and showcase the incredible biodiversity and cultural heritage of the **Blue Ridge Mountains**. With no billboards, commercial traffic, or fast food chains in sight, it offers a tranquil driving experience that favors scenic pull-offs, hiking trails, mountain overlooks, and charming towns. Known as **"America's Favorite Drive,"** the Parkway winds through **lush forests**, **foggy ridges**, and **vibrant meadows**, climbing to elevations over 6,000 feet and offering access to a treasure trove of natural beauty. Along the way, travelers encounter waterfalls, historic farms, Appalachian music centers, and panoramic vistas that stretch across multiple states.

Day 1 - Directions – Blue Ridge Parkway: Afton to Roanoke

Total Distance: ~120 miles
Estimated Time: 4h 30min (without extended stops)

1. **Start at Afton Mountain / Rockfish Gap Entrance**
   Location: Near the junction of US-250 and I-64, by Shenandoah National Park's southern terminus.
2. **Turn onto the Blue Ridge Parkway South (Milepost 0).**
   Begin driving southwest on the Parkway.
3. **Continue past Humpback Rocks Visitor Center and Farm (Milepost 5.8).**
   Optional stop: Short trails and pioneer farm museum.
4. **Drive past Ravens Roost Overlook (Milepost 10.7).**
   Breathtaking views of the Shenandoah Valley.
5. **Continue on the Parkway through Reeds Gap and Love, VA.**
   Stay straight — no turns, just follow the parkway signs.
6. **Pass by Yankee Horse Ridge (Milepost 34.4).**
   Small waterfall nearby, great for quick breaks.
7. **Drive through Tye River Gap and over the Tye River (Milepost 27.2–36).**
   Remain on the Parkway — avoid any junctions with US-60 or VA-56.
8. **Pass Irish Creek Overlook and continue south.**
   Scenic forested sections through George Washington National Forest.
9. **Continue through Otter Creek area (Milepost 60–63).**
   Optional stop: Otter Creek Visitor Center and James River Bridge (low elevation).
10. **Pass through the James River area (Milepost 63.8).**
    Climb back into the mountains after crossing the river.
11. **Keep heading south to Peaks of Otter (Milepost 85.9).**
    Large parking area, restrooms, and lodge. Worth a visit!
12. **After Peaks of Otter, continue driving south.**
    Optional stops: Sharp Top and Abbott Lake.
13. **Approaching Roanoke — watch for the Mill Mountain Spur.**
14. **At Milepost 120.4, exit right onto Mill Mountain Parkway.**
    Follow signs for Roanoke/US-220.
15. **Follow Mill Mountain Parkway for 4 miles downhill.**
16. **At the roundabout, take the exit onto Jefferson Street SE (US-221 North).**
17. **Continue straight into downtown Roanoke, VA.**

Recommended RV Campground for Overnight Stay: Explore Park (Blue Ridge Parkway Milepost 115): 56 Roanoke River Parkway, Roanoke, VA 24014 Phone: +1 540-427-1800 Website: https://www.roanokecountyparks.com/

What to Do on Day 1

- **Hiking:** Try the **Humpback Rocks Trail** (moderate) for sweeping mountain vistas.
- **Wildlife Viewing:** Watch for deer and black bears especially near Otter Creek and Peaks of Otter.
- **Picnicking:** Designated picnic areas at many overlooks; pack lunch for scenic midday stops.
- **Cultural Stop:** The restored **Johnson Farm at Peaks of Otter** offers insight into 19th-century mountain life.

Recommended Fuel Stops (for RVs)

Location	Services Available	Notes
Waynesboro, VA (before entry)	Pilot Travel Center (2416 Rosser Ave)	Full diesel, propane, dump station, large turn radius
Buena Vista, VA (exit US-60 E, 10 min off Parkway)	Exxon / Sheetz	Fuel, restrooms, food — ideal midway refuel
Bedford, VA (near Peaks of Otter exit)	Love's Travel Stop (Route 460)	Diesel, propane, dump station, overnight parking
Roanoke, VA	Various: Love's, Sheetz, Kroger Fuel Centers	Several urban refuel spots, depending on entry point

Key Stops & Scenic Highlights

Milepost	Stop Name	Description
5.8	Humpback Rocks Visitor Center	Trails, picnic area, historic farm buildings
10.7	Ravens Roost Overlook	Dramatic views over the Shenandoah Valley
34.4	Yankee Horse Ridge	Small waterfall trail — short, scenic stretch
60–63	Otter Creek / James River	Visitor Center, bridge, picnic areas — lowest Parkway elevation
85.9	Peaks of Otter	Lake, visitor center, restrooms, scenic trails
120.4	Mill Mountain Parkway Exit	Spur road down to Roanoke, near Mill Mountain Star

Scenic Notes for RV Travelers

- The road is narrow and winding — **stay alert on curves**, and **observe pull-off areas for photography or letting faster vehicles pass**.
- **Low clearance is rarely an issue**, but longer rigs should avoid exploring side roads.
- Expect **no gas stations directly on the Parkway** — plan detours ahead for fueling.
- Cell reception may be **spotty or nonexistent** in higher elevations — download maps offline.
- **Watch for deer** and fog, especially early morning near mountain gaps.

Day 2 - From Roanoke to Blowing Rock, NC

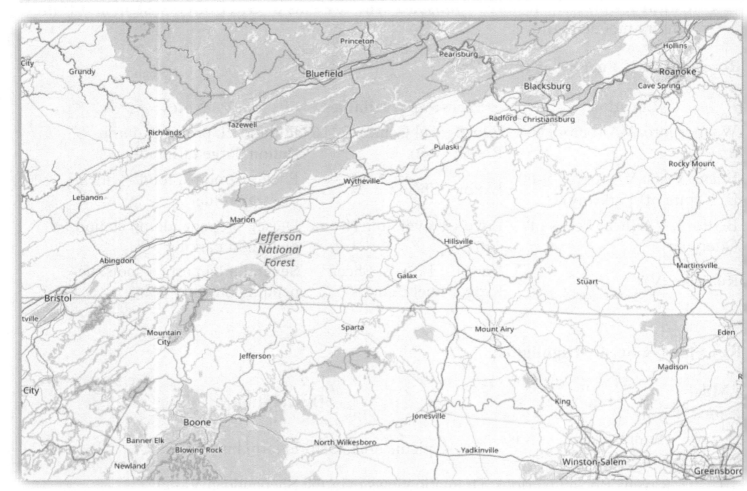

Blue Ridge Parkway Directions: (~172 miles, 5–6 hours)

1. Start in downtown Roanoke, VA on Jefferson Street SE (US-221 South).

2. After approximately 1 mile, follow signs for Mill Mountain Parkway and Blue Ridge Parkway.
3. Turn left onto Mill Mountain Parkway.

4. Continue for 4 miles and merge with Blue Ridge Parkway at Milepost 120.4, heading south.
5. Pass Explore Park Access near Milepost 121.
6. Continue past Stewarts Knob Overlook at Milepost 124.
7. Continue through Back Creek area and over Roanoke River.
8. Pass Smart View Overlook at Milepost 135.9.
9. Continue past Rocky Knob Visitor Center at Milepost 167.1.
10. Continue past Rock Castle Gorge and Rocky Knob Campground.
11. Pass Mabry Mill at Milepost 176.1.
12. Continue south past Groundhog Mountain at Milepost 189.
13. Continue through Fancy Gap, VA at Milepost 199.4.
14. Remain on the Parkway entering North Carolina near Milepost 217.
15. Continue through Cumberland Knob Recreation Area at Milepost 218.
16. Continue past Doughton Park area between Mileposts 240 and 245.
17. Continue past Mahogany Rock Overlook and Alligator Back Overlook.
18. Continue past E.B. Jeffress Park at Milepost 271.
19. Pass Tompkins Knob and Cascades Trail access.
20. Continue past Raven Rocks Overlook at Milepost 289.5.
21. Exit right at Milepost 291.9 for US 221/Blowing Rock.
22. Turn right onto US-221 South.
23. Continue 3 miles into Blowing Rock, NC

Recommended Campground for Overnight Stay

Julian Price Campground: *Blue Ridge Parkway, Milepost 297, near Blowing Rock, NC*

Key Stops & Scenic Highlights

Location	Description	Miles from Roanoke (MP 120.4)
Stewarts Knob Overlook	Wooded overlook offering peaceful views near Explore Park.	3.6
Smart View Overlook	Popular stop with picnic areas and short trails through Appalachian forest.	15.5
Rocky Knob Visitor Center	Interpretive center with access to hiking trails and scenic valleys.	46.7
Mabry Mill	Most photographed site on the Parkway	55.7
Groundhog Mountain	Observation tower and historic wooden fences	68.6

Fancy Gap	Charming mountain community with views and roadside markets.		79.0
Cumberland Knob Recreation Area	First Parkway recreational area with hiking and picnic areas.		96.6
Doughton Park	Extensive trails, meadows, and wildlife viewing		119.6
Mahogany Rock Overlook	Expansive views westward to the Blue Ridge Plateau.		124.6
E.B. Jeffress Park	Short trail to Cascades waterfall		150.6
Raven Rocks Overlook	Dramatic rock formations and sweeping valley views.		169.1
Exit for Blowing Rock	Exit for the charming town of Blowing Rock, NC.		171.5

Location	Fuel Stop		Address	Notes
Roanoke	VA	Sheetz Gas Station	1215 Hershberger Rd NW, Roanoke, VA 24012	Full-service station with diesel, convenience store, and restrooms.
Floyd	VA (via detour from Parkway)	Exxon	200 E Main St, Floyd, VA 24091	Accessible small-town station with snacks and restrooms.
Sparta	NC (via detour from Parkway)	Shell	710 S Main St, Sparta, NC 28675	Reliable stop before rejoining Parkway.
Blowing Rock	NC	Circle K	8416 Valley Blvd, Blowing Rock, NC 28605	Final fuel stop at destination.

Day 3 - From Blowing Rock, NC to Cherokee, NC

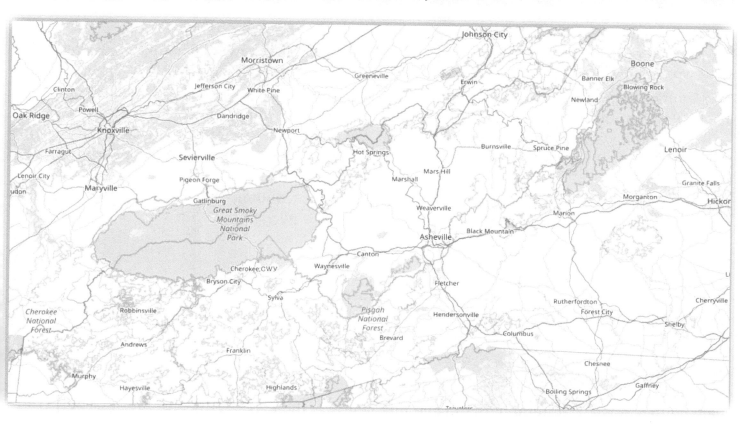

Blue Ridge Parkway Directions: Blowing Rock, NC to Cherokee, NC

Total Distance: ~250 miles
Estimated Time: ~6 hours (excluding stops)

1. Start in Blowing Rock, NC on US-221 South.
2. Merge onto Blue Ridge Parkway at Milepost 291.9.
3. Pass Thunder Hill Overlook (MP 290.4), Julian Price Memorial Park (MP 297.0), and Cone Manor (MP 294.1).
4. Continue to Linn Cove Viaduct (MP 304.4), a dramatic curved bridge along the mountainside.
5. Drive past Grandfather Mountain Overlook (MP 306.6) and Beacon Heights Overlook (MP 305.2).
6. Pass through Linville Falls Area and the Linville Falls Visitor Center (MP 316.4).
7. Continue past Chestoa View Overlook (MP 320.8) and Craggy Gardens (MP 364.4).
8. Approach Little Switzerland (MP 334–338), a winding, scenic tunnel area.
9. Drive by Mount Mitchell State Park access (MP 355.4), Craggy Gardens Visitor Center (MP 364.4), and Craggy Pinnacle Tunnel (MP 364.1).
10. Arrive at the Folk Art Center near Asheville (MP 382).

11. Stay on the Parkway through Asheville, passing Blue Ridge Parkway Headquarters (MP 384).
12. Continue south to Pisgah Inn / Mount Pisgah (MP 408.6), a popular rest and lunch stop.
13. Pass through Pisgah National Forest, including Graveyard Fields (MP 418.8) and Devil's Courthouse (MP 422.4).
14. Continue past Richland Balsam Overlook (MP 431.4), the highest point on the Parkway.
15. Head toward Cherokee, passing Waterrock Knob (MP 451.2) and Big Witch Overlook (MP 461.9).
16. At Milepost 469.1, the Blue Ridge Parkway ends at US-441 near the Oconaluftee Visitor Center in Cherokee, NC.
17. Continue into Cherokee town center if needed.

Recommended Campground for Overnight Stay: Smokemont Campground – Great Smoky Mountains National Park

📍 107 Park Headquarters Road, Cherokee, NC 28719 ☎ +1 (877) 444-6777

Location	Description	Approx. Location
Oconaluftee Visitor Center	Cultural museum and info center at the Parkway's end. Elk sightings common.	Milepost 469.1 / US-441 junction
Mingus Mill	Historic 1886 gristmill still operational. Worth a quick detour.	Just off US-441, near Visitor Ctr
Blue Ridge Parkway End Sign	Perfect photo opportunity to mark completion of the route.	Right where Parkway meets US-441
Big Witch Overlook	Final scenic overlook before reaching Cherokee. Mountain views and tranquility.	Milepost 461.9
Waterrock Knob	High-elevation overlook with a short but steep hike and panoramic views.	Milepost 451.2

Category	Details
Fuel Stops	Best to fill up before leaving Asheville or Maggie Valley. Few options directly on the Parkway.
Rest Areas	Pisgah Inn (MP 408), Waterrock Knob (MP 451), Oconaluftee Visitor Center (MP 469)
Food/Markets	Pisgah Inn Restaurant, Maggie Valley diners, Cherokee eateries

Elevation Alert	Highest Parkway point – Richland Balsam (6,053 ft). Prepare for cooler weather.
Connectivity	Cell signal is limited; download offline maps or bring printed directions.

End-of-Route

- The final leg from Blowing Rock to Cherokee transitions from **cool mountain vistas** to **lush forest valleys**, weaving through **Pisgah National Forest** and **Great Smoky Mountains National Park**.
- Expect multiple **tunnels**, winding curves, and dramatic elevation changes.
- The **highest point on the entire Blue Ridge Parkway**, **Richland Balsam Overlook (MP 431.4)**, offers a memorable stop for reflection and photos.
- Once in Cherokee, you're in the heart of **Cherokee Nation** territory, a great place to explore **Native American heritage**, **local crafts**, and **riverside trails**.

THE GREAT RIVER ROAD

The Great River Road: An Iconic Journey Along the Mississippi

The Great River Road is one of America's most storied scenic byways, stretching over 2,000 miles along the majestic Mississippi River. Beginning at the river's humble source in Lake Itasca, Minnesota, and winding all the way to the Gulf of Mexico in Louisiana, this route offers travelers a unique chance to experience the heart of America — its history, cultures, landscapes, and towns — all tied together by the powerful current of the Mississippi.

Established in 1938, the Great River Road is not a single highway, but rather a network of local, state, and federal roads that trace the river through ten states. As you journey southward, you'll pass through charming river towns, vibrant cities, lush farmlands, mysterious bayous, and historic battlefields. From the bluffs of Minnesota and Wisconsin to the musical soul of Memphis, the plantations of Mississippi, and finally the Cajun spirit of Louisiana, this road is more than a path — it's a living story of America's soul. Whether you're an RV adventurer, a road tripper with a camera in hand, or simply a traveler hungry for new experiences, the Great River Road offers both scenic beauty and cultural depth. Along the way, you'll find countless museums, interpretive centers, state parks, wildlife refuges, and welcoming communities, all ready to share their corner of the river with you. This route isn't about getting there fast — it's about soaking in every mile of history, nature, and local flavor.

Great River Road: Key Facts & Numbers

- **Total Length:** Approx. **3,000 miles (4,800 km)**
- **Established: 1938**
- **States Crossed: 10** (Minnesota, Wisconsin, Iowa, Illinois, Missouri, Kentucky, Tennessee, Arkansas, Mississippi, Louisiana)
- **Starting Point: Lake Itasca State Park, Minnesota**
- **Ending Point: Venice, Louisiana (at the Gulf of Mexico)**
- **Main River Followed: Mississippi River**

Designations & Recognitions

- **National Scenic Byway**: Designated in several sections
- **All-American Road**: Certain parts recognized for exceptional natural and cultural qualities
- **Marked with:** Green and white pilot's wheel signs with river imagery

Route Structure

- **Not one continuous road**, but a **collection of state, county, and federal highways**
- Includes **historic U.S. highways, backroads, and rural routes**
- Follows the **Mississippi River Trail (MRT)** in many biking-accessible sections

Day 1 - From Clearwater County to La Crosse, WI

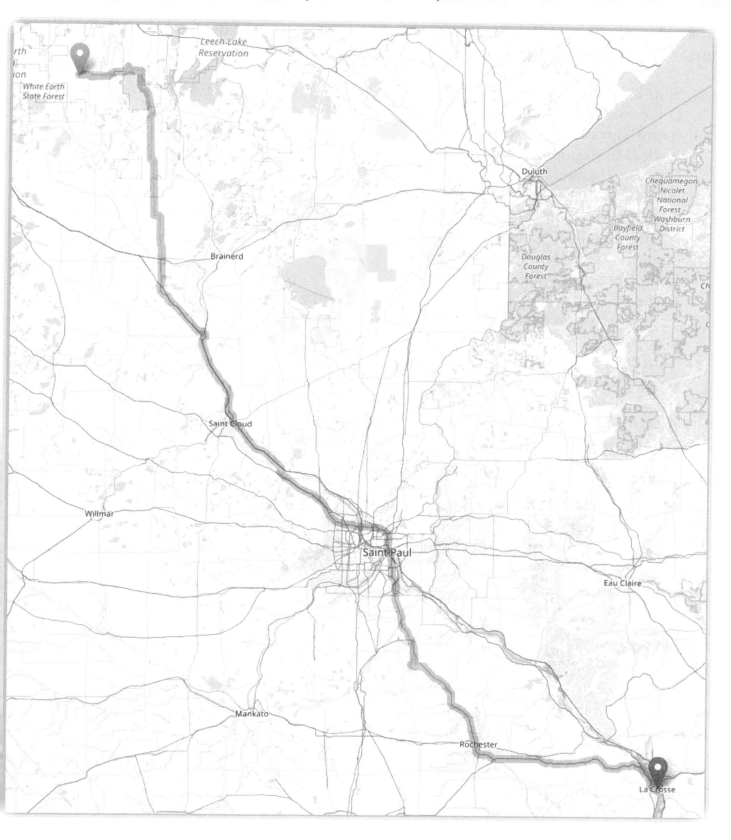

Directions –Total Distance: ~609 km (~378 miles) Estimated Driving Time: ~8 hours

1. Start in Clearwater County, MN.
2. Drive south on County Road 2 and follow signs to **Lake Itasca State Park** (Mississippi River headwaters).
3. Exit the park and head east on **MN-200 East**.
4. Turn left onto **MN-92 East**.
5. Continue on **MN-92 East** and merge onto **MN-71 North** toward **Bemidji**.
6. Enter **Bemidji** via **Paul Bunyan Drive SE**, following **US-2 East**.
7. Continue east on **US-2** through **Cass Lake** toward **Deer River**.
8. Turn right onto **US-169 South** at **Grand Rapids**.
9. Continue through **Hill City** and **Aitkin**, staying on **US-169 South**.
10. In **Onamia**, take a short detour west to visit **Mille Lacs Lake**, then return to US-169.
11. Continue on **US-169 South** to **Milaca**, then merge onto **MN-23 West**.
12. At **Foley**, turn left onto **MN-25 South** toward **Little Falls**.
13. Enter **Little Falls** via **Lindbergh Drive South**.
14. Stop at **Charles A. Lindbergh State Park**.
15. Head east on **MN-27 East** to **Royalton**, then merge onto **US-10 East** toward **St. Cloud**.
16. In **St. Cloud**, exit onto **MN-23 East**.
17. Cross the **Mississippi River** and continue on **MN-23 East** toward **Milaca**.
18. Follow **MN-23 East** to **US-169 South**, but take **local riverside roads** if available, to stay closer to the river (optional).
19. Enter the **Twin Cities area** via **I-94 East**.
20. In **Minneapolis–St. Paul**, merge onto **MN-61 South** (Great River Road).
21. Follow **US-61 South** through **Hastings**, **Red Wing**, **Lake City**, and **Wabasha**.
22. After **Wabasha**, cross the **Mississippi River** into Wisconsin via the **Wabasha–Nelson Bridge**.
23. Continue south on **WI-35 South** (Great River Road) through **Alma**, **Fountain City**, and **Trempealeau**.
24. Stay on **WI-35 South** and arrive in **La Crosse, WI**.

Campground	Location	Amenities
Itasca State Park Campground	Lake Itasca, MN	Full hookups, showers, dump station, hiking trails
Bemidji KOA Journey	Bemidji, MN	Water/electric/sewer, Wi-Fi, laundry, pool
Charles A. Lindbergh State Park	Little Falls, MN	Electric hookups, restrooms, near historic sites
Pettibone Resort RV Park	La Crosse, WI	Full hookups, riverfront sites, showers, fishing access
Attraction	**Location**	**Description**

Mississippi Headwaters	Lake Itasca State Park	Start of the Mississippi River, scenic walking trail
Paul Bunyan & Babe the Blue Ox	Bemidji, MN	Iconic photo stop with folklore statues
Barn Bluff	Red Wing, MN	Hiking trail with panoramic river views
Great River Bluffs State Park	La Crescent, MN	Blufftop overlooks of Mississippi River Valley

Fuel Stops:

🔘 **Stop 1: Bemidji, MN (~95 miles)**
Holiday Stationstores, 2025 Paul Bunyan Dr SE, Bemidji, MN 56601

🔘 **Stop 2: Grand Rapids, MN (~190 miles)**
Holiday Stationstores, 2030 S Pokegama Ave, Grand Rapids, MN 55744

🔘 **Stop 3: St. Cloud, MN (~285 miles)**
Kwik Trip, 6250 County Rd 120, St. Cloud, MN 56303

🔘 **Stop 4: Red Wing, MN (~355 miles)**
Kwik Trip, 727 Main St, Red Wing, MN 55066

Day 2 - From La Crosse, WI to Dubuque, IA

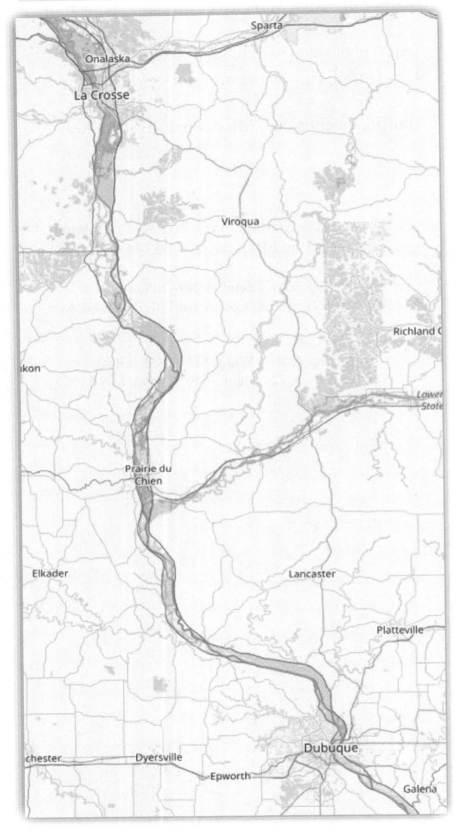

Directions – Total Distance: ~165 miles | Estimated Driving Time: ~4.5 hours

1. Start in downtown La Crosse, WI.
2. Head south on US-14/US-61 out of La Crosse, following signs for the Great River Road.
3. Continue on US-61 South for approximately 9 miles to reach Stoddard, WI.
4. Stay on US-61 South and drive 7 miles to Genoa, WI.
5. Continue on US-61 South for another 12 miles to Ferryville, WI.
6. Proceed on US-61 South for 14 miles and arrive in Prairie du Chien, WI.
7. Cross the Mississippi River via the US-18 West bridge into Marquette, IA.
8. Continue on US-18 West briefly, then turn left onto IA-76 North to visit Effigy Mounds National Monument (optional detour of ~3 miles).
9. Return south on IA-76 to Marquette, then turn right to join US-52 South (Great River Road).
10. Follow US-52 South for 24 miles, driving along scenic bluffs, until you reach Guttenberg, IA.
11. Stay on US-52 South from Guttenberg and continue approximately 42 miles through small river towns and forested areas.
12. Arrive in Dubuque, IA via the northern entrance to the city on US-52.

Campground	Location	Features	Miles from La Crosse	Notes
Blackhawk Park	De Soto, WI	Electric hookups, restrooms, river view, fishing	24	Scenic riverside location, peaceful
Pikes Peak State Park	McGregor, IA	Electric hookups, hiking trails, river overlooks	65	Popular park with overlooks and trails
Nelson Dewey State Park	Cassville, WI	Electric sites, hiking trails, Indian mounds	93	Historic setting, bluff views
Grant River Recreation Area	Potosi, WI	Paved roads, level sites, river access	105	Quiet and well-maintained riverside site

Attraction	Location	Description	Miles from La Crosse	Notes
Effigy Mounds National Monument	Harpers Ferry, IA	Animal-shaped Native American mounds, hiking trails, river views	67	Unique mound shapes, peaceful hiking
Eagle Point Park	Dubuque, IA	Panoramic river views, pavilions, public park on a bluff	165	Top view of Dubuque and the river
Lock and Dam No. 11	Dubuque, IA	River navigation structure, educational viewing area	165	Great for watching boats and locks

Station	Location	Miles from La Crosse	Notes
Kwik Trip	506 Cass St, La Crosse, WI 54601	0	Central La Crosse, good for starting out
Casey's General Store	1923 S Marquette Rd, Prairie du Chien, WI 53821	42	Quick stop before crossing into Iowa
BP	102 S Highway 52, Guttenberg, IA 52052	92	Mid-route fill-up in small town
Kwik Stop	4039 Pennsylvania Ave, Dubuque, IA 52002	165	Full service near journey's end

What You'll See:

As you make your way from **La Crosse to Dubuque** along the Great River Road, the scenery gently shifts from lively riverfront neighborhoods to quiet, rural landscapes lined with bluffs and forests. The small towns of **Stoddard**, **Genoa**, and **Ferryville** give you a feel for the slow pace and simple charm of life along the Mississippi. One of the key highlights is **Prairie du Chien**, a town steeped in history and a perfect place to take a longer break. From there, crossing the river into Iowa brings a sense of transition, with the twin towns of **Marquette and McGregor** welcoming you on the other side. A short detour leads to **Effigy Mounds National Monument**, where ancient burial sites shaped like animals are nestled among scenic trails with sweeping river views. Continuing south on **US-52**, the road winds beautifully through forested hills and along river bends. The town of **Guttenberg** offers one of the most picturesque river walks on the route, with well-preserved buildings and peaceful views. As you approach **Dubuque**, the landscape opens up again. You'll descend from bluffs into a city that blends its historic river roots with modern attractions, making for a grand and scenic finish to your drive.

Day 3 – From Dubuque, IA to **Quincy, IL**

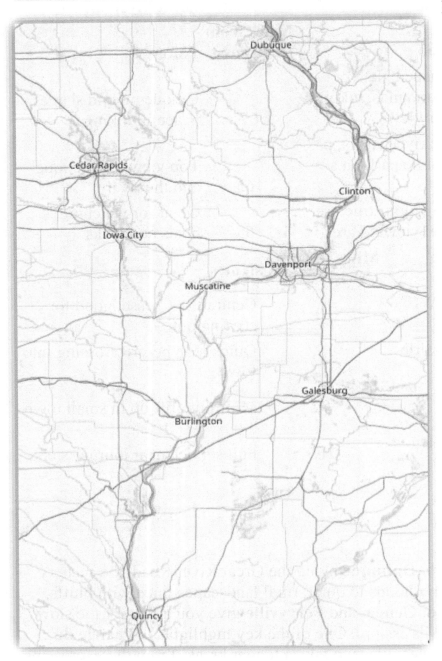

Directions – Total Distance: ~180 miles | Estimated Driving Time: ~5 hours

1. Start in Dubuque, IA. Cross the Mississippi River into Illinois via the Julien Dubuque Bridge, taking US-20 East.
2. Enter East Dubuque, IL and continue briefly on US-20 East.
3. Turn right onto IL-35 South, then merge onto IL-84 South. This road is part of the official Great River Road and leads you into Galena, a historic town known for its preserved 19th-century architecture.
4. Stay on IL-84 South and drive along the Mississippi River until you reach Savanna, IL. This stretch offers several scenic river views.
5. In Savanna, take US-52 East / IL-64 East across the Mississippi River into Sabula, IA—an island town in the middle of the river.
6. Drive through Sabula and then cross back into Illinois via the Savanna-Sabula Bridge, returning to Savanna, and continue south on IL-84.
7. Proceed through the towns of Thomson and Cordova, staying on

IL-84 South as you follow the river closely.

8. Reach East Moline and continue through the Quad Cities via IL-92 East and then rejoin IL-84 South in Rock Island.
9. Exit Rock Island and continue south through Andalusia and into the rural sections of western Illinois, still following IL-84 and the Great River Road.
10. Continue south until you reach Nauvoo, IL. Take time to visit the Nauvoo Historic District, where restored 1800s buildings recall the town's early Mormon history.
11. From Nauvoo, continue south on IL-96, following the river through Hamilton.
12. Near Hamilton, look for Lock & Dam No. 19, a major engineering structure on the Mississippi.
13. Stay on IL-96 South, driving through rolling countryside and small towns as you approach Quincy.
14. Arrive in Quincy, IL, a city known for its riverfront parks, historic homes, and vibrant downtown overlooking the Mississippi.

Campground	Location	Distance from Dubuque	Services	Notes
Spruce Creek Park Campground	Bellevue, IA	~13 miles	Electric hookups, restrooms, river access	Quiet, scenic site with fishing and river views.
Blanding Landing Recreation Area	Hanover, IL	~30 miles	Electric sites, restrooms, picnic areas	Nestled in nature, peaceful setting.
Thomson Causeway Recreation Area	Thomson, IL	~55 miles	Electric sites, restrooms, hiking trails	Located on a river peninsula, very scenic.
Fisherman's Corner Recreation Area	Hampton, IL	~70 miles	Electric hookups, restrooms, fishing area	Great spot for birdwatching and relaxing.
Nauvoo State Park	Nauvoo, IL	~120 miles	Electric sites, restrooms, hiking trails	Close to the Nauvoo Historic District.
Siloam Springs State Park	Clayton, IL	~160 miles	Electric sites, restrooms, fishing lake	Wooded, quiet park with nature trails.

Scenic Points and Major Attractions

- **Eagle Point Park** (Dubuque, IA): Panoramic views of the Mississippi River and Lock & Dam No. 11 from a high bluff. Great spot for photos and picnics.

- **Bellevue State Park** (Bellevue, IA): Overlooks the river valley with wooded trails and wildlife viewing areas.
- **Nauvoo Historic District** (Nauvoo, IL): Explore restored 1800s buildings, historic sites, and cultural landmarks from early Mormon settlers.
- **Great River Trail sections** (Thomson to Rock Island, IL): Ideal for biking or walking alongside the river.
- **Lock & Dam No. 19** (Hamilton, IL): Impressive navigation structure along the river, worth a brief stop.

Station	Location	Notes
Kwik Star	Dubuque, IA	Convenient spot to fuel up at the start of the day.
Casey's General Store	Bellevue, IA	Good for gas and a quick bite.
Shell	Clinton, IA	Full-service stop with snacks and restrooms.
BP	Nauvoo, IL	Handy fuel stop before or after exploring Nauvoo.
Quincy Travel Plaza	Quincy, IL	Large station with fuel, food, and rest area facilities.

Day 4 – From Quincy, IL to St. Louis, MO

Directions – Total Distance: ~135 miles | Estimated Driving Time: ~3 hours

1. Start in Quincy, IL.
2. Head south on IL-57 South, following the signs for the Great River Road.
3. Continue on IL-57 South for about 15 miles until you reach Fall Creek, IL.
4. Enjoy scenic views of the Mississippi River as you drive through rural and wooded areas.
5. Stay on IL-96 South for approximately 25 miles until you arrive in Kampsville, IL.
6. In Kampsville, take the Kampsville Ferry to cross the Illinois River.
7. After the ferry crossing, continue on IL-100 South for about 20 miles until you reach Hardin, IL.
8. This stretch offers spectacular views of the bluffs and river valleys.
9. From Hardin, continue south on IL-100 for about 25 miles to reach Grafton, IL.
10. Grafton is a charming river town known for its wineries and recreational activities along the water.
11. Stay on IL-100 South for another 15 miles until you reach Alton, IL.
12. Alton features several historic landmarks and scenic overlooks of the Mississippi River.

13. From Alton, continue south on IL-3 for approximately 30 miles to East St. Louis, IL.
14. This part of the drive takes you through industrial and urban zones along the river.
15. Cross the Mississippi River into St. Louis, MO, using either the Martin Luther King Bridge or the Eads Bridge.

16. Both bridges provide iconic views of the St. Louis skyline and the famous Gateway Arch.
17. Arrive in St. Louis, MO.

18. Welcome to St. Louis! Take time to explore the city's many attractions, including Gateway Arch National Park, the Missouri Botanical Garden, and the City Museum.

Traveling the **Great River Road** from **Quincy, IL** to **St. Louis, MO** offers a wealth of experiences, from scenic landscapes to historical landmarks. Here's a guide to RV campgrounds, scenic viewpoints, notable attractions, and fuel stations along this route:

RV Campgrounds:

1. **Pere Marquette State Park** (Grafton, IL): Located near the confluence of the Mississippi and Illinois Rivers, this park offers RV-friendly campsites with picturesque river views. It's an ideal spot for hiking, fishing, and eagle watching during winter months.
2. **St. Louis N.E. / I-270 / Granite City KOA Journey** (Granite City, IL): Situated just 12 miles from downtown St. Louis, this campground provides full hookups, a swimming pool, and easy access to city attractions, including the Gateway Arch.

Scenic Viewpoints:

- **Meeting of the Great Rivers Scenic Overlook** (Grafton, IL): Experience panoramic views where the Mississippi and Illinois Rivers converge. This area is renowned for its breathtaking sunsets and is part of the 33-mile scenic byway.

- **Piasa Park** (Alton, IL): Home to the legendary Piasa Bird mural, this park offers a unique blend of natural beauty and folklore, overlooking the Mississippi River.

Attractions and Landmarks:

- **Gateway Arch National Park** (St. Louis, MO): Standing at 630 feet, the iconic Gateway Arch symbolizes the westward expansion of the United States. Visitors can take a tram ride to the top for expansive city views.
- **Malcolm W. Martin Memorial Park** (East St. Louis, IL): This park features the Gateway Geyser, which mirrors the height of the Gateway Arch, and offers an elevated platform for unparalleled views of the St. Louis skyline.
- **Route 66 State Park** (Eureka, MO): Delve into the history of the famed "Mother Road" with exhibits showcasing Route 66 memorabilia. The park also offers trails and picnic areas along the Meramec River.

Fuel Stations: Quincy, IL: Multiple fuel stations are available along IL-57 as you commence your journey southward.

- **Alton, IL**: As a larger city along the route, Alton offers numerous refueling options, especially along IL-100.

Day 5 – From St. Louis, MO to Memphis, TN

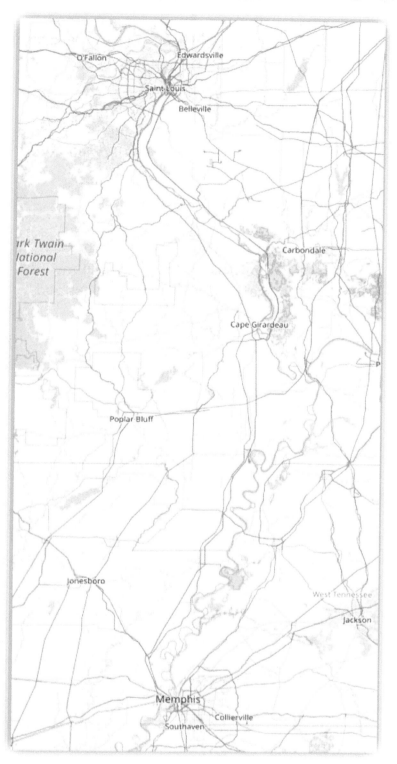

Total Distance: ~280 miles (450 km)
Estimated Driving Time: ~6 to 6.5 hours

1. Begin in St. Louis, MO. Cross the Mississippi River into Illinois via the Eads Bridge or Martin Luther King Bridge to commence your journey on the Great River Road.
2. Upon entering Illinois, merge onto Illinois Route 3 (IL-3) South, also designated as the Great River Road.
3. Proceed south on IL-3 through the towns of Cahokia and Dupo, continuing for approximately 30 miles until you reach Chester, IL.
4. In Chester, cross the Chester Bridge back into Missouri, entering the town of Perryville.
5. From Perryville, take Missouri Route 51 (MO-51) South for about 10 miles to connect with U.S. Route 61 (US-61) South, a primary component of the Great River Road.
6. Continue on US-61 South, passing through Jackson and Cape Girardeau, for roughly 50 miles until you arrive in Sikeston, MO.
7. In Sikeston, merge onto Interstate 55 (I-55) South, which closely parallels the Mississippi River and is part of the Great River Road in this region.
8. Follow I-55 South for approximately 47 miles, crossing into Arkansas, and continue for another 55 miles until you reach West Memphis, AR.
9. From West Memphis, cross the Hernando de Soto Bridge over the Mississippi River into Memphis, TN, concluding your journey along this segment of the Great River Road.

RV Campgrounds:

1. **Tom Sawyer's RV Park (West Memphis, AR):** Situated directly on the banks of the Mississippi River, this campground provides spacious sites with full hookups, allowing guests to watch the river traffic from their RVs. Amenities include laundry facilities and walking trails.
2. **Sundermeier RV Park (St. Charles, MO):** Located near St. Louis, this park offers paved sites with full hookups and is in proximity to local attractions and the Katy Trail.
3. **Cahokia RV Parque (Cahokia, IL):** Conveniently close to St. Louis attractions, this campground provides full hookups and a friendly staff.

Scenic Viewpoints:

- **Pere Marquette State Park (Grafton, IL):** Known for its breathtaking views of the Illinois River, this park offers hiking trails that lead to scenic overlooks, showcasing the confluence of the Illinois and Mississippi Rivers.
- **Chester Welcome Center (Chester, IL):** Perched atop a bluff overlooking the Mississippi River, this spot provides panoramic views of the river and the surrounding landscape.

Notable Attractions:

- **Gateway Arch National Park (St. Louis, MO):** Standing at 630 feet, the iconic Gateway Arch symbolizes the westward expansion of the United States. Visitors can take a tram ride to the top for expansive city views.
- **Popeye Statue (Chester, IL):** Chester, the birthplace of Popeye's creator, features a statue of the beloved cartoon character, celebrating the town's unique contribution to pop culture.
- **National Civil Rights Museum (Memphis, TN):** Located at the Lorraine Motel, the site of Dr. Martin Luther King Jr.'s assassination, this museum offers a deep and moving exploration of the American civil rights movement.

Fuel Stations:

- **St. Louis, MO:** Numerous fuel stations are available throughout the city, especially near major highways and interstates.
- **Cape Girardeau, MO:** As a mid-sized city along the route, Cape Girardeau offers multiple refueling options conveniently located near the highway.
- **Sikeston, MO:** Known for its hospitality, Sikeston provides several fuel stations, including those suitable for larger RVs.
- **Memphis, TN:** A major urban center, Memphis has a plethora of fuel stations, particularly near interstate exits and within the city.

General Notes: Reservations: It's advisable to book campsites in advance, especially during peak travel seasons, to ensure availability. **Local Events:** Check local tourism websites for festivals or events that might coincide with your visit, enhancing your travel experience. **Road Conditions:** Stay updated on road conditions or construction along the Great River Road to ensure a smooth journey.

Day 6 – From Memphis, TN to Vicksburg, MS

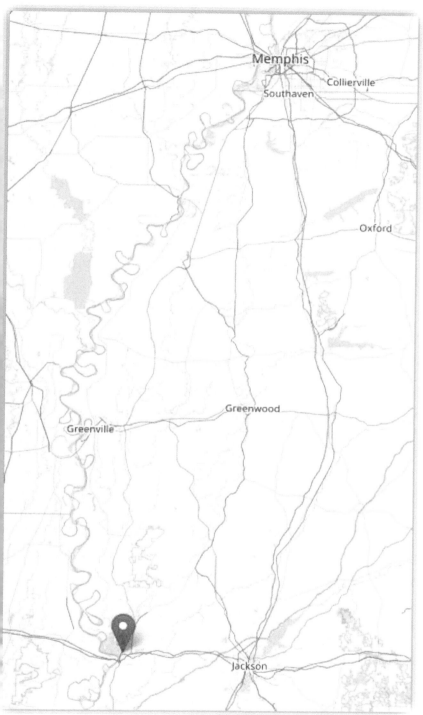

Total Distance: ~240 miles
Estimated Driving Time: ~6 hours (excluding stops)

1.　Start in Memphis, TN. Begin your journey downtown near the Mississippi River, heading south on US Highway 61 (US-61), which serves as the primary route for the Great River Road through this region.
2.　Enter Mississippi. Continue on US-61 South for approximately 12 miles, crossing into Mississippi.
3.　Proceed through Tunica, MS. Drive about 40 miles south on US-61 to reach Tunica, known for its casinos and the Gateway to the Blues Museum.
4.　Continue to Clarksdale, MS. Stay on US-61 South for another 40 miles to arrive in Clarksdale, famed for its rich blues heritage and the Delta Blues Museum.
5.　Head towards Cleveland, MS. Maintain your course on US-61 South for approximately 35 miles to reach Cleveland, home to the GRAMMY Museum Mississippi.
6.　Proceed to Greenville, MS. Continue south on US-61 for about 35 miles to Greenville, where you can explore the Hebrew Union Temple Museum and the 1927 Flood Museum.
7.　Continue to Leland, MS. Drive approximately 8 miles on US-61 South to Leland, the birthplace of Jim Henson and home to the Birthplace of Kermit the Frog Museum.
8. Head towards Vicksburg, MS. Continue on US-61 South for about 70 miles to reach Vicksburg, renowned for the Vicksburg National Military Park and its significant Civil War history.

RV Campgrounds:

1. **Tunica Recreation Area** (Tunica, MS): Situated approximately 40 miles south of Memphis along US-61, this campground offers RV sites with essential hookups. Its proximity to the Mississippi River provides campers with serene views and fishing opportunities.

2. **Delta Village RV Park** (Clarksdale, MS): Located about 75 miles from Memphis, this park serves as an excellent base for exploring Clarksdale's rich blues heritage. Amenities include full hookups, laundry facilities, and easy access to local attractions.

3. **Greenville Campground** (Greenville, MS): Roughly 120 miles into your journey, this campground offers spacious RV sites with full hookups. Its location near the Mississippi River allows for picturesque sunsets and leisurely walks along the levee.

4. **Ameristar RV Park** (Vicksburg, MS): Conveniently located near the Ameristar Casino, this RV park provides full-service sites. At approximately 200 miles from Memphis, it marks a comfortable end to your day's journey, with dining and entertainment options nearby.

Scenic Viewpoints & Attractions: Tunica RiverPark & Museum (Tunica, MS): This facility offers panoramic views of the Mississippi River and delves into the region's history through interactive exhibits. It's an ideal spot to stretch your legs and immerse yourself in the river's storied past. **Delta Blues Museum** (Clarksdale, MS): Dedicated to preserving the history of the blues, this museum showcases artifacts and exhibits related to legendary musicians. A must-visit for music enthusiasts keen on understanding the roots of this influential genre. **Winterville Mounds** (Greenville, MS): This ancient Native American site features ceremonial mounds dating back over a millennium. The on-site museum provides insights into the indigenous cultures that once thrived along the Mississippi.

- **Vicksburg National Military Park** (Vicksburg, MS): Commemorating a significant Civil War battle, this park offers driving tours, monuments, and a restored ironclad gunboat. It's a poignant reminder of the area's historical significance.

Notable Statues & Landmarks: The Crossroads (Clarksdale, MS): Marked by a guitar sculpture at the intersection of Highways 61 and 49, this iconic site is steeped in blues lore, famously associated with Robert Johnson's legendary pact.

Fuel Stations: Love's Travel Stop (Walls, MS): Located about 20 miles south of Memphis along US-61, this station offers ample space for RVs, fueling options, and a selection of travel essentials. **Circle K** (Clarksdale, MS): Situated approximately 75 miles from Memphis, this station provides standard fueling services and a convenience store for snacks and beverages. **Shell Station** (Greenville, MS): Around 120 miles into your journey, this station offers diesel and gasoline options, along with a well-stocked convenience store. **Pilot Travel Center** (Vicksburg, MS): Near the culmination of your trip, this facility caters to larger vehicles, providing multiple fueling bays, dining options, and rest areas.

Day 7 – From Vicksburg, MS to Baton Rouge, LA

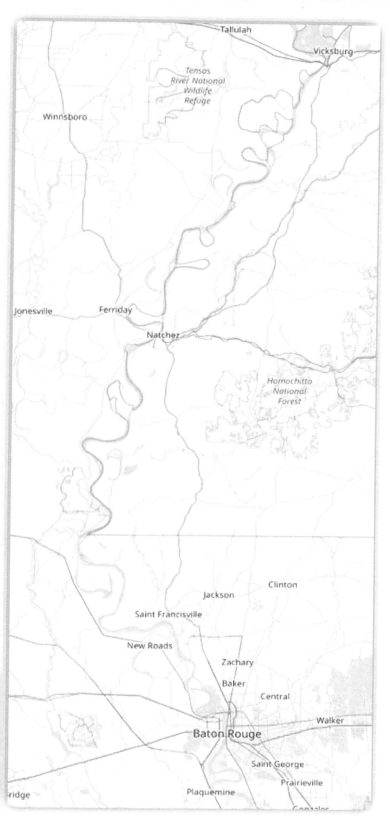

Total Distance: ~150 miles (241 km)
Estimated Driving Time: ~3.5 to 4 hours (without long stops)

1. **Start in Vicksburg, MS.** Begin your journey downtown near the Mississippi River, heading south on **US Highway 61 (US-61)**, which serves as the primary route for the Great River Road through this region.
2. **Proceed through Port Gibson, MS.** Drive approximately 28 miles south on US-61 to reach Port Gibson, known for its historic sites and antebellum architecture.
3. **Continue to Natchez, MS.** Stay on US-61 South for about 40 miles to arrive in Natchez, one of the oldest cities on the Mississippi River, renowned for its well-preserved antebellum homes and rich history.
4. **Cross into Louisiana.** From Natchez, cross the Mississippi River via the Natchez-Vidalia Bridge into Vidalia, Louisiana.
5. **Head towards St. Francisville, LA.** Continue south on US-61 for approximately 50 miles to reach St. Francisville, a town celebrated for its historic plantations and charming downtown area.
6. **Arrive in Baton Rouge, LA.** Proceed on US-61 South for about 30 miles to enter Baton Rouge, the capital city of Louisiana, offering a blend of cultural attractions, including the Louisiana State Capitol and various museums.

Campground Name	Location	Distance from Vicksburg	Notes
River Town Campground	Vicksburg, MS	0 miles	Full hookups; spacious sites; approximately 5 miles off I-20 at exit 1B.
The Joshua On Hwy 61	Woodville, MS	~90 miles	Located off US Highway 61; offers 30 and 50 amp electrical hookups, water, and sewer connections.
Farr Park RV Campground	Baton Rouge, LA	~150 miles	Situated by the Mississippi River; part of a larger equestrian park; offers water and electric hookups with a dump station.

Scenic Viewpoints & Attractions:

- **Windsor Ruins** (Port Gibson, MS): Approximately 30 miles south of Vicksburg, these hauntingly beautiful columns are remnants of a grand antebellum mansion, offering a glimpse into the region's storied past.
- **Natchez Trace Parkway** (Near Natchez, MS): This historic forest trail extends roughly 440 miles from Natchez to Nashville, TN. The section near Natchez provides scenic drives, hiking trails, and insights into early American history.
- **Rosedown Plantation State Historic Site** (St. Francisville, LA): About 120 miles from Vicksburg, this well-preserved plantation offers guided tours of the main house and gardens, showcasing antebellum architecture and Southern horticulture.

- **Louisiana State Capitol** (Baton Rouge, LA): Standing as the tallest capitol building in the U.S., visitors can enjoy panoramic views of Baton Rouge from its observation deck and explore its rich history.

Statues & Notable Landmarks:

- **Forks of the Road Slave Market Site** (Natchez, MS): This poignant site marks one of the largest slave markets in the South, with informative markers detailing its historical significance.
- **Port Hudson National Cemetery** (Zachary, LA): A solemn landmark commemorating soldiers who fought in the Civil War's longest siege, offering a reflective stop along your journey.

Fuel Station	Location	Miles from Vicksburg	Notes
Shell	4747 Highway 61 S, Vicksburg, MS	5	South of Vicksburg on US-61, offers premium fuel options
Circle K (Vicksburg)	574 Hwy 61 N, Vicksburg, MS	0	Located in Vicksburg, convenient for early fuel stop

Murphy USA	Natchez, MS	65	Budget-friendly pricing, convenient stop
Pilot Travel Center	St. Francisville, LA	120	Spacious for RVs, diesel available, food options
Circle K (Baton Rouge)	13315 Old Hammond Hwy, Baton Rouge, LA	150	Urban station with full traveler services

Day 8 – From Baton Rouge, LA to New Orleans, LA

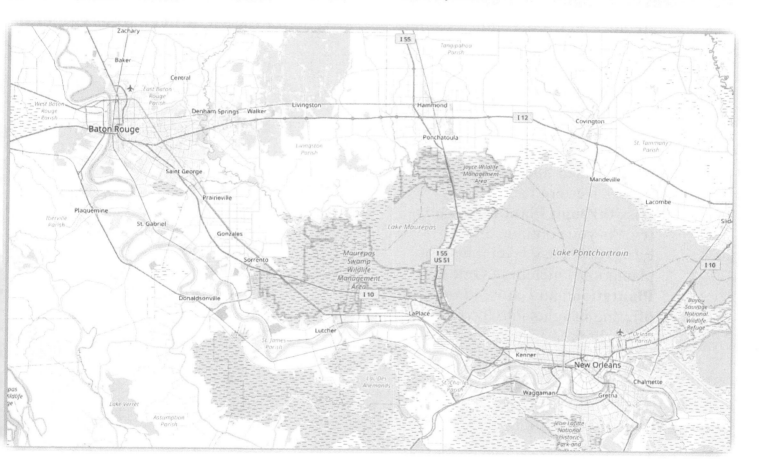

Total Distance: ~90 miles (145 km)
Estimated Driving Time: ~2 to 2.5 hours

1. **Start in Baton Rouge, LA.** Begin your journey downtown near the Mississippi River, heading east on **Government Street (LA-73)**.
2. **Merge onto River Road (LA-327).** Continue east on Government Street and turn right onto **River Road (LA-327)**, which closely follows the Mississippi River's eastern bank.
3. **Proceed through Plaquemine, LA.** Drive approximately 15 miles

south on LA-327 to reach **Plaquemine**, a historic town known for the **Plaquemine Lock State Historic Site**.

4. **Continue on LA-1 South.** From Plaquemine, merge onto **LA-1 South**, continuing along the river's eastern bank.

5. **Cross the Mississippi River at Donaldsonville, LA.** After about 20 miles on LA-1 South, cross the **Sunshine Bridge (LA-70)** to reach **Donaldsonville**, located on the river's western bank.

6. **Follow LA-18 (River Road) East.** In Donaldsonville, turn left onto **LA-18 East**, also known as **River Road**, which traces the Mississippi River's western bank.

7. **Pass through Plantation Country.** As you continue on LA-18 East, you'll pass several historic plantations, including **Oak Alley Plantation** and **Laura Plantation**, offering insights into the region's antebellum history.

8. **Cross back to the eastern bank at Gramercy, LA.** At **Gramercy**, use the **Veterans Memorial Bridge (LA-3213)** to cross the Mississippi River back to the eastern bank.

9. **Continue on LA-44 East.** After crossing the bridge, turn right onto **LA-44 East (River Road)**, following the river's eastern bank.

10. **Proceed through Reserve and LaPlace, LA.** Continue on LA-44 East through the towns of **Reserve** and **LaPlace**, known for their rich Creole and Cajun heritage.

11. **Merge onto US-61 South (Airline Highway).** In LaPlace, merge onto **US-61 South**, also known as **Airline Highway**, heading towards New Orleans.

12. **Arrive in New Orleans, LA.** Continue on US-61 South for approximately 25 miles to enter **New Orleans**, where you can explore the city's vibrant culture, music, and cuisine

Fuel Station	Location	Miles from Baton Rouge	Notes
Shell - Plaquemine	Plaquemine, LA	15	Convenient fuel stop on River Road
Chevron - Donaldsonville	Donaldsonville, LA	35	Near bridge crossing, snacks and diesel available
Circle K - LaPlace	LaPlace, LA	75	Large station with amenities near US-61
Exxon - New Orleans	New Orleans, LA	90	Urban stop near downtown, good access for large vehicles

Campground	Location	Miles from Baton Rouge	Notes
Farr Park RV Campground	Baton Rouge, LA	0	Located along the river, with full hookups and access to equestrian trails
Poche Plantation RV Park	Convent, LA	45	Historic setting with plantation views and full RV facilities
Bayou Segnette State Park	Westwego, LA (near New Orleans)	85	Spacious park near the city with hookups, trails, and bayou access
French Quarter RV Resort	New Orleans, LA	90	Premium RV resort in the heart of New Orleans, walking distance to the French Quarter

Landmark / Scenic Point	Location	Miles from Baton Rouge	Notes
Plaquemine Lock State Historic Site	Plaquemine, LA	15	Historic lock with a museum and river views
Oak Alley Plantation	Vacherie, LA	50	Famous antebellum plantation with oak-lined entry
Laura Plantation	Vacherie, LA	52	Creole plantation with guided heritage tours
St. Joseph Plantation	Vacherie, LA	53	Family-run plantation with preserved original structures
French Quarter & Jackson Square	New Orleans, LA	90	Historic district with architecture, music, and local culture

FLORIDA KEYS SCENIC HIGHWAY

Route Length: ~110 miles
Driving Time: ~3–4 hours (without stops)
Route: From **Key Largo** to **Key West** along **U.S. Route 1 (Overseas Highway)**
Designation: National Scenic Byway & All-American Road

Introduction

Few road trips in America feel as surreal, sun-drenched, and soul-lifting as the drive through the Florida Keys. The **Florida Keys Scenic Highway**, also known as the **Overseas Highway**, is more than a route — it's a ribbon of road stretched across aquamarine water, linking a tropical chain of coral islands with 42 bridges and an endless parade of postcard-perfect views. This legendary stretch of **U.S. Route 1** runs from the top of the Keys in **Key Largo** all the way down to the vibrant streets of **Key West**, the southernmost point in the continental United States. But it's not just about getting from Point A to Point B — it's about soaking in the salty breeze, spotting dolphins leaping from the Gulf, and stopping whenever your instincts (or your appetite for key lime pie) tell you to.

For RV travelers, this is paradise on pavement. With plenty of **oceanfront campgrounds**, **pull-offs for scenic photos**, and small towns full of color and character, the route is designed for slow travel. Whether you're in it for the sunsets at **Seven Mile Bridge**, the snorkeling at **Bahia Honda State Park**, or the quirky charm of **Key West**, the Florida Keys Scenic Highway delivers unforgettable memories at every mile marker. This chapter will guide you mile by mile down this iconic highway, with **campgrounds**, **fuel stops**, **attractions**, and **hidden gems** tailored to RV travelers. So top off your tank, roll down the windows, and let the island time take over.

Directions:

1. Start at the northern gateway to the Florida Keys Scenic Highway in **Key Largo, FL**, at the intersection of Card Sound Road and U.S. Route 1 (MM 110).

2. Head southwest on **US-1 South (Overseas Highway)** toward Tavernier.
3. Pass through **Tavernier**, continuing on US-1 South for approximately 10 miles.
4. Drive through **Islamorada**, known as the "Village of Islands"; enjoy ocean views and roadside attractions.
5. Continue on US-1 South through **Lower Matecumbe Key**, crossing several small bridges with panoramic water views.
6. Cross the **Channel 5 Bridge**, one of the taller spans on the highway, offering excellent ocean scenery.
7. Enter **Long Key**, and pass **Long Key State Park** at approximately MM 67.5.
8. Drive through **Layton**, a quiet community on Long Key.
9. Cross over **Conch Key** and continue onto **Duck Key**, connected via the **Tom's Harbor Cut Bridge**.
10. Continue on US-1 South to **Marathon**, the midpoint of the Keys and home to shops, fuel, and groceries.
11. Just past Marathon, prepare to cross the iconic **Seven Mile Bridge**, beginning around MM 47.
12. Cross **Seven Mile Bridge**, the longest segment on the Overseas Highway, connecting **Knight's Key** to **Little Duck Key**.
13. Continue through **Bahia Honda Key**, passing **Bahia Honda State Park** at MM 37.
14. Cross into **Big Pine Key**, known for the **National Key Deer Refuge**.
15. Continue on US-1 South through **Cudjoe Key**, **Sugarloaf Key**, and **Big Coppitt Key**, passing scenic waterways and smaller islands.
16. Reach **Stock Island**, just before entering Key West.
17. Cross the final bridge into **Key West**, the end point of the scenic byway.
18. Continue along **US-1 South** until it terminates at the **Southernmost Point Marker** on Whitehead Street, near the corner of South Street — the official end of U.S. Route 1 and the Florida Keys Scenic Highway.

RV Campgrounds:

1. **John Pennekamp Coral Reef State Park** – Key Largo, MM 102.5
   Oceanfront campsites, snorkeling access, full hookups. Excellent starting point.
2. **Fiesta Key RV Resort & Marina** – Long Key, MM 70
   Large resort with ocean views, marina, and full amenities.
3. **Jolly Roger RV Resort** – Marathon, MM 59
   Family-friendly park with affordable rates and full services.
4. **Bahia Honda State Park Campground** – Big Pine Key, MM 37
   Stunning beachside RV spots, very popular – book early!
5. **Boyd's Key West Campground** – Key West, MM 5
   Closest full-service RV campground to downtown Key West.

Scenic Points & Attractions

1. **African Queen Canal Cruise** – Key Largo, MM 100

Cruise on the famous steamboat from the classic film.

2. **History of Diving Museum** – Islamorada, MM 83
   Fascinating exhibits on deep-sea diving history.
3. **Seven Mile Bridge Scenic Lookout** – Marathon, MM 47
   Iconic photo stop with sweeping ocean views.
4. **Bahia Honda State Park** – Bahia Honda Key, MM 37
   White sand beaches, snorkeling, hiking trails.
5. **Southernmost Point Buoy** – Key West, MM 0
   Legendary landmark and popular photo op.

Fuel Stations (RV Accessible)

1. **Circle K** – Key Largo, MM 102
   Easy access for RVs, convenience store attached.
2. **Chevron** – Islamorada, MM 82
   Good mid-route stop for fuel and snacks.
3. **Valero** – Marathon, MM 54
   Easy pull-through layout for larger RVs.
4. **Shell** – Big Pine Key, MM 30
   Clean restrooms, diesel available.
5. **Chevron** – Stock Island, MM 5
   Last big fuel stop before entering Key West.

BEARTOOTH HIGHWAY

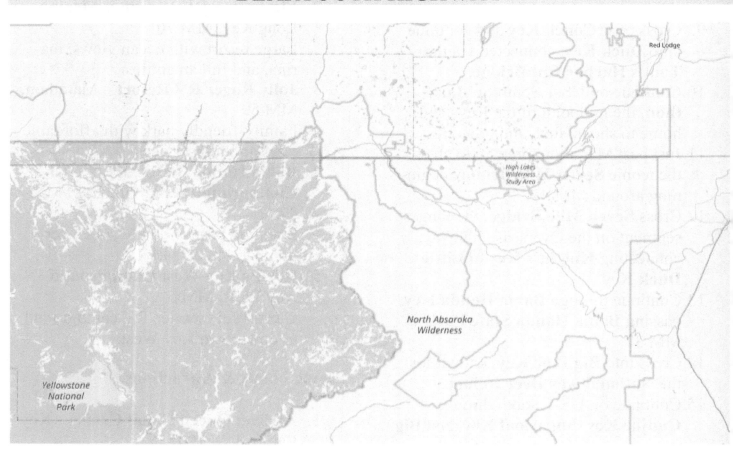

Beartooth Highway

Length: ~68 miles (109 km)
Route: Red Lodge, Montana → Cooke City, Montana (near the Northeast Entrance of Yellowstone National Park)
Highest Point: Beartooth Pass – 10,947 ft (3,337 m)
Season: Typically **open from late May to mid-October** (weather permitting)
Designation: All-American Road & National Scenic Byway
Highway Number: U.S. Route 212

Directions:

1. Begin in **Red Lodge, Montana** at the intersection of Broadway Avenue and U.S. Route 212.
2. Head **southwest on US-212 West**, following signs for **Beartooth Highway / Cooke City**.
3. Exit the town limits and begin ascending into the **Beartooth Mountains**.
4. Continue through a series of **steep switchbacks** for approximately 12 miles.
5. Stop at **Rock Creek Vista Point** (around mile marker 47), a large scenic overlook with restrooms and panoramic views.
6. Resume driving **uphill** toward the **Beartooth Plateau**, passing several turnouts with views of alpine valleys and snowfields.
7. Reach the **Beartooth Pass summit** at **10,947 feet (3,337 meters)** — the highest point on the route.
8. Begin descending along **US-212 West**, following signs toward **Cooke City**.
9. Drive past a series of **glacial lakes**, including **Gardner Lake**, **Twin Lakes**, and **Long Lake**, with occasional scenic pullouts.
10. Enter a short stretch of **northern Wyoming**, remaining on US-212 — the road curves through high mountain meadows and cliffs.
11. Re-enter **Montana** as you approach **Silver Gate**, a small alpine village with cabins, lodges, and cafés.
12. Continue west on US-212 for the final 4 miles to **Cooke City, Montana**.
13. Arrive at the **junction of US-212 and US-296**, the official **western end of the Beartooth Highway**.
14. From here, continue 4 miles further on US-212 to reach the **Northeast Entrance of Yellowstone National Park**, if desired.

Introduction

Regarded by many as **"the most beautiful drive in America,"** the **Beartooth Highway** is a dramatic, high-altitude journey through the rugged Northern Rockies. Winding its way through the **Beartooth and Absaroka Mountain ranges**, this 68-mile route climbs to nearly 11,000 feet above sea level, delivering a breathtaking alpine experience that's as challenging as it is unforgettable.

Starting in the charming western town of **Red Lodge, Montana**, the highway quickly ascends into a world of **glacial lakes, snowfields, wildflower meadows**, and **sweeping switchbacks**. At the summit — **Beartooth Pass** — you're standing on top of the world, with panoramic views that stretch for miles in every direction. From there, the road dips and rises again through wild, unspoiled terrain before reaching **Cooke City**, a remote outpost nestled just outside the **northeast**

entrance to Yellowstone National Park. For many travelers, this drive is not just a way to reach Yellowstone — it's the highlight of the entire trip.

Technical Driving Notes for RV Travelers

- **Road Type:** 2-lane paved mountain highway with tight curves, steep grades, and high elevation
- **Steepest Sections:** 6–8% grades; numerous switchbacks near the summit
- **Vehicle Restrictions:** No formal bans on RVs or trailers, but **large rigs should proceed with caution**
- **Fuel:** No fuel between **Red Lodge** and **Cooke City** – **fill up before you start**
- **Weather:** Conditions can change rapidly; snow is possible even in July.
- **Cell Coverage:** Limited to none along much of the route — download offline maps ahead of time

Highlights Along the Way

- **Rock Creek Vista Point:** A designated overlook offering safe pullouts and dramatic cliffside views.
- **Beartooth Plateau:** One of the highest and most extensive alpine plateaus in North America.
- **Glacial Lakes & Hikes:** Dozens of trailheads and pullouts for quick hikes or photo ops.
- **Wildlife:** Keep an eye out for mountain goats, marmots, moose, and even grizzly bears.
- **Alpine Flora:** During late spring and early summer, wildflowers bloom across the high meadows.

Why It's Special

The Beartooth Highway isn't about speed — it's about **immersion**. It's a rare place where **you feel the road climbing through ecosystems**, from dense pine forests to wind-blasted tundra. You don't just observe the mountains here — you live in them, even if only for an hour or two.

For RV travelers, this is a **bucket-list drive** — thrilling, humbling, and filled with wonder. If your vehicle can handle the curves and the altitude, **the Beartooth Highway is one of the finest examples of why we hit the road in the first place.**

Campground	Location	Type	Notes
Red Lodge KOA Journey	Red Lodge, MT	Private RV Park with hookups	Full amenities, good base before ascent
Parkside Campground	Near Vista Point, MT	USFS campground (no hookups)	Close to Rock Creek Vista Point
Beartooth Lake Campground	Near Beartooth Lake, WY	USFS campground (no hookups)	Alpine setting near scenic lakes
Fox Creek Campground	East of Cooke City, WY	Primitive campground	Quiet, first-come first-serve sites

Colter Campground	Silver Gate, MT	Small forest campground	Near Cooke City with forest access
Pebble Creek Campground	Inside Yellowstone NP (near NE entrance)	NPS campground (RV-friendly)	Great for staging Yellowstone entry

Landmark / Attraction	Location	Highlights
Rock Creek Vista Point	Near mile 47	Panoramic views, restrooms, large parking
Gardner Lake Overlook	Beartooth Pass area	Small lake set in high alpine basin
Beartooth Pass Summit	10,947 ft elevation	Highest point on the highway with 360° views
Twin Lakes Viewpoint	Near highway descent	Scenic mountain lakes, photo ops
Beartooth Plateau	Mid-route alpine section	Expansive alpine tundra above tree line
Cooke City Montana Museum	Cooke City, MT	Local history of miners and pioneers

Fuel Station	Location	Notes
Cenex Red Lodge	MT	Red Lodge, MT
Top of the World Store (limited fuel)	Highway midpoint, WY	Very limited fuel, check ahead
Cooke City Sinclair	Cooke City, MT	Reliable last-stop station before Yellowstone
Silver Gate General Store	Silver Gate, MT	Small fuel stop, seasonal availability

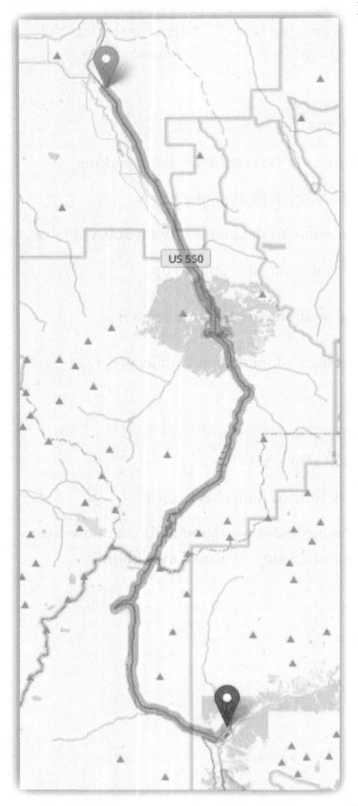

Million Dollar Highway

Route Length: ~25 miles (40 km)
Route: From **Ouray, CO** to **Silverton, CO**, along **U.S. Route 550**
Elevation Gain: Up to **11,018 feet** at **Red Mountain Pass**
Known for: Dramatic cliffs, narrow lanes, no guardrails, and jaw-dropping alpine views
Season: Open year-round (weather permitting), but **caution advised in winter**

Introduction

The **Million Dollar Highway** is one of America's most iconic mountain drives — and one of the most daring. Carved into the side of the **San Juan Mountains** in southwestern Colorado, this 25-mile stretch of **U.S. Route 550** connects the historic mining towns of **Ouray** and **Silverton** through a corridor of staggering beauty — and serious adrenaline. Though its name's origin is debated — some say it refers to the **cost of construction**, others to the **"million-dollar views"**, or even the **gold ore embedded in the gravel** — what's not in question is its legend. With **steep drop-offs**, **no guardrails**, and **tight mountain curves**, this road is not for the faint of heart. But for those behind the wheel of an RV or van, it's an unforgettable experience that feels like driving through the very spine of the Rockies. You'll climb over **Red Mountain Pass** at 11,018 feet, pass old mining structures rusting on the hillsides, and weave through alpine tundra that seems more Swiss Alps than Southwest U.S. Despite the challenge, RVers continue to seek it out — especially during **fall foliage season**, when the mountains explode in gold.

Directions:

1. Start in **downtown Ouray, Colorado**, heading south on **U.S. Route 550 South**.
2. Exit the town limits and begin climbing immediately into the **San Juan Mountains**.
3. Follow the narrow two-lane road as it hugs the cliffside with **no guardrails** — stay alert and keep your speed slow.
4. Drive past **Bear Creek Falls**, where a stone bridge carries the highway over a plunging mountain waterfall. There is a small pullout for photos.
5. Continue along a series of **tight curves and steep grades**, ascending toward **Red Mountain Pass**.
6. Pass remnants of **historic mining sites**, including the **Yankee Girl Mine**, visible from the road.
7. Reach the summit at **Red Mountain Pass**, elevation **11,018 feet (3,358 m)** — the highest point on the Million Dollar Highway.
8. Begin your descent, navigating winding downhill stretches with limited shoulder space.
9. Continue south through **dense forested sections and alpine meadows**, with dramatic drop-offs still on the roadside.
10. Enter the **Animas River Valley** as the terrain begins to open up.
11. Arrive at the northern edge of **Silverton, Colorado**, a historic mining town with dirt streets, shops, and scenic rail connections.
12. End your journey in **downtown Silverton**, where U.S. 550 intersects with local roads — fuel, dining, and lodging are available here.

Campground	Location	Type	Notes
4J+1+1 RV Park & Campground	Ouray, CO	Private RV campground with full hookups	Walking distance to downtown Ouray
Amphitheater Campground	Just above Ouray, CO	USFS, tent & small RV sites, no hookups	Stunning views above Ouray
Moler Campground	Red Mountain Pass area	Primitive USFS campground	Basic mountain campground, remote
Red Mountain RV Park	South of Red Mountain Pass	Small RV park with basic services	Tight access, scenic location
Silverton Lakes RV Resort	Silverton, CO	Private RV resort, full services	Great amenities in town
Kendall Campground	Near Silverton, CO	USFS, first-come-first-serve	Popular for boondocking near river

Landmark / Attraction	Location	Highlights
Bear Creek Falls Overlook	Highway overlook just south of Ouray	Waterfall flowing beneath the highway

Red Mountain Pass Summit	Summit of the Million Dollar Highway	Panoramic alpine views at 11,018 ft
Yankee Girl Mine	Visible from highway before Silverton	Well-preserved mining structure
Idarado Mine Overlook	Interpretive stop on US-550	Historic signs & valley viewpoint
Silverton Historic District	Downtown Silverton	1880s architecture, shops, cafes
Ouray Box Canyon Falls Park	West side of Ouray	Short hike and roaring waterfall

Fuel Station	Location	Notes
Conoco – Ouray	Ouray, CO	Last full-service station before heading south
Silverton Gas (formerly Exxon)	Silverton, CO	Reliable fuel in Silverton

SKYLINE DRIVE (SHENANDOAH NATIONAL PARK)

Skyline Drive Directions (North to South)

Total Distance: 105 miles (169 km)
Estimated Driving Time (without stops): ~3.5 hours
Speed Limit: 35 mph throughout the park

1. Begin at the **Front Royal Entrance Station** (mile 0), heading south on Skyline Drive.
2. Continue past **Dickey Ridge Visitor Center** at mile 4.6; this is your first opportunity for maps, restrooms, and park info.
3. Drive through a series of gentle curves and forests; enjoy early overlooks like **Gooney Run** and **Hogback Mountain** (mile ~20).
4. At **mile 22.1**, you'll reach **Mathews Arm Campground** on the west side, the northernmost RV-accessible campground.
5. Proceed past **Elkwallow Wayside** around mile 24 for fuel (seasonal), food, and restrooms.
6. Stay on Skyline Drive through **Marys Rock Tunnel** at mile 32.2; this tunnel has a 12'8" height clearance.
7. At mile 41.7, reach **Skyland Resort**, a popular place to stop for meals, lodging, and scenic views.

8. Shortly after, visit **Stony Man Trailhead** and **Crescent Rock Overlook** for short hikes and wide-angle views.
9. At mile 51, enter **Big Meadows Area** — this is the heart of the park, with a lodge, visitor center, and gas station.
10. Just beyond is **Big Meadows Campground** at mile 51.2, the most RV-friendly campground along Skyline Drive.
11. Continue south and pass **Lewis Mountain** around mile 57.5, a smaller campground ideal for a quieter stay.
12. As you drive further, watch for **Bearfence Mountain** at mile 56.4 and **Baldface Mountain Overlook** at mile 61.2.
13. Near mile 79.5, you'll reach **Loft Mountain Campground**, the largest in the park and offering stunning ridge views.

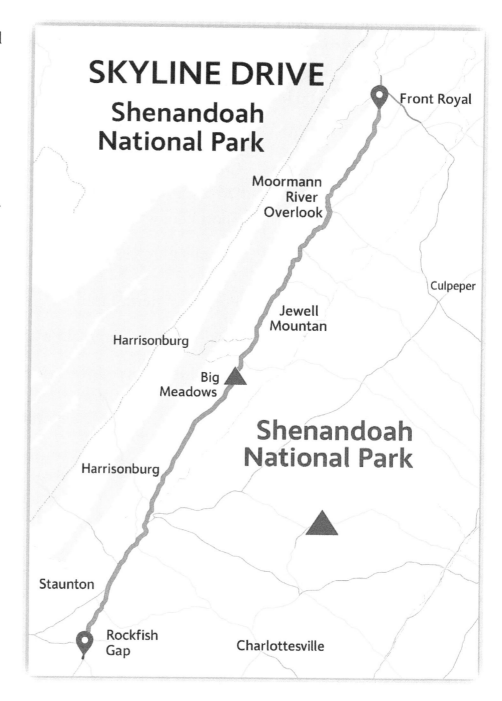

14. Continue south through the final leg of the drive with scattered pull-offs and valley vistas.

15. Arrive at the **Rockfish Gap Entrance Station** (mile 105), marking the end of Skyline Drive. This location connects directly to the **Blue Ridge Parkway**.

Attraction / Over-look	Mile Marker	Highlights
Gooney Run Over-look	6.8	Early view of Massanutten Range
Hogback Overlook	20.8	Longest panoramic view in the park
Marys Rock Tunnel	32.2	Drive-through tunnel carved in granite
Stony Man Trail	41.7	Short hike with top views
Crescent Rock Over-look	44.4	Broad valley views near Skyland
Dark Hollow Falls Trail	50.7	Popular waterfall trail
Bearfence Mountain	56.4	Moderate rock scramble with 360° view
Baldface Mountain Overlook	61.2	Peaceful overlook with wide ridgeline

Campground	Mile Marker	RV Access	Notes
Mathews Arm Campground	22.1	Yes	Northernmost campground, wooded area
Big Meadows Campground	51.2	Yes, best for RVs	Most popular, near visitor center and fuel
Lewis Mountain Campground	57.5	Limited	Quiet, smaller sites, best for vans or small RVs
Loft Mountain Campground	79.5	Yes, scenic ridge sites	Spacious, dramatic views, dump station available

Location	Mile Marker	Services	Notes
Elkwallow Wayside	24.0	Fuel (seasonal), groceries, restrooms	Northern fuel point – open seasonally
Big Meadows Way-side	51.2	Fuel, groceries, café, restrooms	Full-service mid-park stop, RV-friendly

GOING-TO-THE-SUN ROAD (GLACIER NATIONAL PARK)

GOING-TO-THE-SUN ROAD – Navigation Directions (West to East)

1. Start in West Glacier, MT, near the Glacier National Park west entrance.
2. Enter the park at West Glacier Entrance Station and continue straight on Going-to-the-Sun Road.
3. Drive along the western shore of Lake McDonald for approximately 10 miles.
4. Pass Lake McDonald Lodge on your left. Continue heading northeast.
5. After crossing McDonald Creek, begin ascending through the forested terrain toward Avalanche Creek.
6. Pass Avalanche Campground and Trail of the Cedars (optional scenic stop).
7. Continue climbing toward The Loop, a large switchback curve with scenic mountain views.
8. Navigate the tight curves and continue ascending through alpine terrain.
9. Reach the Weeping Wall, where water cascades directly onto the road from a cliff face.

10. Proceed toward Logan Pass, the highest point of the road at 6,646 feet.
11. Stop at the Logan Pass Visitor Center for restrooms, trails, and panoramic views.
12. Begin descending on the eastern side of the divide toward St. Mary Lake.
13. Stop at Jackson Glacier Overlook on the right for a view of one of the park's few visible glaciers.
14. Continue east, passing scenic points like Sunrift Gorge and Wild Goose Island Overlook.
15. Follow the road along the northern shore of St. Mary Lake.

- **Total Distance:** ~50 miles (80 km)
- **Driving Time (without stops):** ~2 to 2.5 hours
- **Start Point: West Glacier Entrance / Apgar Village**
- **End Point: St. Mary Entrance / St. Mary Visitor Center**
- **Highest Elevation: Logan Pass – 6,646 feet (2,026 m)**
- **Open Season:** Late June to mid-October (varies annually based on snow)
- **Speed Limit:** 25–45 mph (strictly enforced)
- **Road Type:** 2-lane paved scenic mountain road, steep grades, sheer drop-offs (no guardrails)

16. Arrive at the St. Mary Visitor Center near the park's eastern entrance.
17. Exit the park onto US-89 in the town of St. Mary, MT.

● **Vehicle Restrictions:** RVs or trailers longer than 21 feet or wider than 8 feet are prohibited beyond Avalanche Creek due to sharp curves and narrow roadways.

Quick Facts & Technical Overview:

- **Tunnel:** One – **East Side Tunnel** (short)
- **Fuel Availability: No gas stations** on the road — fill up at **West Glacier** or **St. Mary**
- **Restrooms:** Available at **Lake McDonald Lodge, Avalanche, Logan Pass, Rising Sun**
- **Camping:** Campgrounds at **Apgar, Avalanche, Rising Sun, St. Mary**
- **Best Time to Drive:** Morning or early evening (low traffic, better light)
- **Cell Signal:** Very limited —
- **Park Pass Required:** Yes – Entry fee or America the Beautiful Pass

Campground	Location	RV Access	Notes
Apgar Campground	West Glacier / Apgar Village	Yes (large sites available)	Largest campground in the park, near Lake McDonald
Avalanche Campground	Near Avalanche Creek	Limited (not for large RVs)	Shaded sites, popular hiking access
Rising Sun Campground	East of Logan Pass, near St. Mary Lake	Moderate (check length restrictions)	Near boat launch and visitor center

St. Mary Campground	East Entrance near St. Mary Visitor Center	Yes (best suited for RVs)	Reservations recommended during peak season

Scenic Spot / Landmark	Location	Highlights
Lake McDonald	West side, near Apgar	Largest lake in the park, kayaking, photography
The Loop	Midway switchback curve	Hairpin turn with broad views
Weeping Wall	Cliffside cascade, west of Logan Pass	Water flows across the road from cliff face
Logan Pass	Highest point, visitor center & trails	Wildlife, Hidden Lake Trail, 360° views
Jackson Glacier Overlook	East side, view of glacier	Best visible glacier from the road
Wild Goose Island Overlook	St. Mary Lake viewpoint	Most photographed spot in Glacier NP
Sunrift Gorge	Short hike to gorge and bridge	Unique geological formation, accessible trail

Fuel Station	Location	Notes
West Glacier Gas	West Glacier, MT	Main station before entering the park westbound
St. Mary Gas Station	St. Mary, MT	Only fuel option near the eastern gate
Canyon Foods Gas (Hungry Horse)	Just west of park entrance	Good for fill-ups before Apgar/Avalanche access

🌲 Interesting Facts & Local Secrets – Going-to-the-Sun Road

- **The road took over two decades to complete** due to the difficulty of building through steep granite mountains and avalanche-prone terrain. It was fully opened in **1933**, and parts were constructed using manual labor and explosives.
- **You can stand on the Continental Divide at Logan Pass**, meaning water from one side flows to the Pacific, and from the other, to the Atlantic. It's a subtle but fascinating geologic divide right beneath your feet.
- **The stonework along the road is original and hand-laid.** The retaining walls (called "guard rocks") are part of the historic architecture and are protected as part of the National Historic Landmark status.

- **Hidden Lake Overlook Trail**, accessed from Logan Pass, is one of the best places in the U.S. to see **mountain goats up close**. They're often found near the boardwalk and overlook, totally unfazed by hikers.
- **The Loop**, a dramatic hairpin turn, is the *only switchback on the entire road*. Its design minimized environmental impact and was chosen for its efficiency at climbing the steep mountain face.
- **Avalanche danger shapes the road's schedule** — every spring, crews spend weeks clearing deep snow and ice, sometimes up to **80 feet deep** in drifts. Plowing the road is one of the most dangerous snow-removal operations in the NPS.
- **Sun Point Nature Trail**, often skipped, offers **multiple waterfalls and lake views** in a single short hike — perfect for RVers short on time but craving a taste of Glacier's backcountry.

US HIGHWAY 101 (OREGON COAST)

Overview:

The **U.S. Highway 101 (Oregon Coast Highway)** runs **north to south** along the **entire Pacific coastline of Oregon**, covering roughly **363 miles (584 km)** from the **Columbia River** at the Washington border down to **Brookings**, just above California.

- **Total Length in Oregon:** ~363 miles
- **Direction:** North → South (most scenic for ocean views on the right)
- **Start: Astoria, OR**
- **End: Brookings, OR**
- **Driving Time:** ~10–12 hours without stops, but best enjoyed over 3–5 days
- **Road Type:** 2-lane coastal highway, with frequent pull-offs, bridges, and tunnels
- **RV-Friendly?** ✔ Yes — heavily used by RVers, with many campgrounds and scenic parking options

Hidden Facts & Unique Insights

- **U.S. 101 wasn't originally designed as a scenic byway.** It began as a commercial trade route linking Oregon's coastal ports and towns. Only in the 1960s did the state begin promoting it for tourism, ultimately becoming the *Pacific Coast Scenic Byway*.

- **The bridges are architectural masterpieces.** Many of the iconic coastal bridges (like the Yaquina Bay Bridge and Siuslaw River Bridge) were designed by **Conde McCullough**, a visionary who believed that bridges should be **both functional and beautiful**.
- **Oregon has the highest concentration of lighthouses on the West Coast.** With 11 historic lighthouses, many like **Heceta Head** are still active and open to visitors, offering jaw-dropping coastal views and even lighthouse B&B stays.
- **The tides completely change the landscape.** Beaches like **Cape Kiwanda** or **Seal Rock** appear massive at low tide but can vanish beneath crashing waves just hours later. Some tide pool explorations are time-sensitive.

Day 1 – U.S. Highway 101 (Astoria, OR → Newport, OR)

Distance: ~135 miles | **Estimated Driving Time:** ~4.5 hours (without stops)

1. Start in downtown **Astoria, OR** at the northern junction of U.S. Highway 101.
2. Head south on **US-101 S** across the **Youngs Bay Bridge**, leaving Astoria behind.

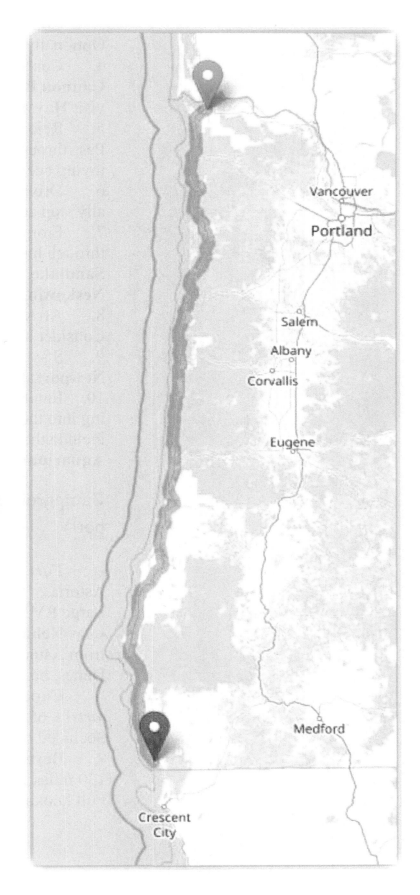

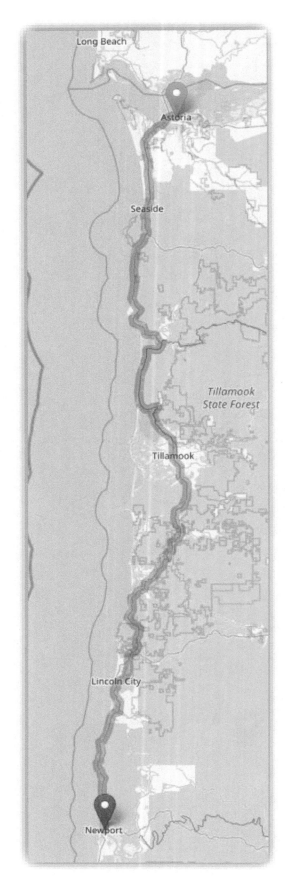

3.   Continue for about 17 miles to reach **Seaside, OR**. Optionally stop at the promenade or beach viewpoint.

4.   Continue on US-101 south for 11 miles to reach **Cannon Beach**. Detour west into town if you'd like to visit **Haystack Rock**.

5.   Rejoin US-101 and continue south for 25 miles. Pass through **Arch Cape**, **Manzanita**, and **Nehalem**, enjoying ocean views and forested curves.

6.   Drive another 20 miles to **Tillamook, OR**. Optionally stop at the **Tillamook Creamery** for lunch or a tour.

7.   From Tillamook, stay on **US-101 S**. Drive 40 miles through lush coastal forests and alongside bays, passing **Sandlake**, **Pacific City (via OR-131 detour)**, and **Neskowin**.

8.   Arrive in **Lincoln City, OR** after roughly 1 hour. Consider a beach stop or shopping break.

9.   Stay on US-101 and drive the final 25 miles to **Newport, OR**.

10.   Enter Newport via **North Coast Highway**, continuing into the historic bayfront area. Recommended stops include the **Yaquina Head Lighthouse**, **Oregon Coast Aquarium**, and **Newport Bayfront**.

Campgrounds Along U.S. 101 (Astoria → Newport)

- **Fort Stevens State Park** – *Astoria* – 0 miles from Astoria
Large RV sites, beach access, historic military fort.
- **Nehalem Bay State Park** – *Manzanita* – 40 miles from Astoria
Dunes, beach and forest setting, RV-friendly.
- **Cape Lookout State Park** – *Tillamook (via Netarts)* – 65 miles from Astoria
Secluded oceanfront camping, great for hiking.
- **Beverly Beach State Park** – *North of Newport* – 130 miles from Astoria
Full hookups, ocean views, ideal for RVs.

Scenic Stops & Attractions

- **Astoria Column** – *Astoria* – 2 miles
  Climb for panoramic views of Columbia River and Pacific.
- **Seaside Promenade** – *Seaside* – 17 miles
  Classic Oregon coast boardwalk and beach access.
- **Haystack Rock** – *Cannon Beach* – 25 miles
  Iconic sea stack with tide pools and photo ops.
- **Neahkahnie Mountain Viewpoint** – *Nehalem* – 35 miles
  One of the best views along the Oregon Coast.
- **Tillamook Creamery** – *Tillamook* – 65 miles
  Cheese tasting, family-friendly, local favorite.
- **Cape Kiwanda** – *Pacific City* – 80 miles
  Huge sand dune, natural sea stacks, coastal views.
- **Devil's Punchbowl** – *Otter Rock* – 120 miles
  Natural sea cave with crashing waves and lookout.

Fuel Stations (RV-Friendly)

- **Astoria 76** – *Astoria, OR* – 0 miles
  Great for a full tank before starting.
- **Chevron Seaside** – *Seaside, OR* – 17 miles
  Quick stop just off the highway.
- **Shell Tillamook** – *Tillamook, OR* – 65 miles
  RV accessible with convenience store.
- **Chevron Lincoln City** – *Lincoln City, OR* – 110 miles
  Located near groceries and services.
- **Texaco Newport** – *Newport, OR* – 135 miles
  Ideal final fill-up near major attractions.

-

Hidden Facts & Local Insights – Day 1: Astoria to Newport

- **Astoria is the oldest American settlement west of the Rockies**, established in 1811. It's also where the **Lewis and Clark Expedition** ended. The **Astoria Column** atop Coxcomb Hill commemorates that epic journey with a spiraling mural carved into its concrete surface.
- **Seaside, Oregon, marks the official end of the Lewis & Clark Trail**. There's a bronze statue of the explorers at the promenade, where they first saw the Pacific Ocean. Many RVers overlook this meaningful historic detail.
- **Cannon Beach's Haystack Rock is part of the Oregon Islands National Wildlife Refuge.** During low tide, you can see colorful sea stars, anemones, and mussels in tidepools — but you're also stepping into a protected marine ecosystem. Watch your footing and don't disturb nesting birds like tufted puffins (yes, puffins!).

- **Between Cannon Beach and Manzanita lies the legend of buried treasure. Arch Cape** and **Neahkahnie Mountain** are tied to 17th-century Spanish sailors rumored to have hidden gold somewhere on the slopes — hikers still search for it today.
- **The "Three Capes Scenic Loop"** is a beautiful alternative to the main highway between **Tillamook** and **Pacific City**. It includes **Cape Meares**, home to Oregon's shortest lighthouse and the bizarre "Octopus Tree," an ancient Sitka spruce with branches like tentacles.
- **Tillamook is more than cheese.** The area has a working **blimp hangar** from World War II that now houses the **Tillamook Air Museum**, one of the largest wooden structures in the world.
- **The Pacific City beach is one of the few places in Oregon where dory boats still launch directly from the sand.** Watching the flat-bottomed fishing boats crash back onto shore is part of the local culture.

Day 2 – U.S. Highway 101 (Newport, OR → Crescent City, CA)

Distance: ~195 miles
Estimated Driving Time: ~5 hours (not including scenic stops)

1. Start in downtown **Newport, OR**, heading south on U.S. Highway 101 from North Coast Highway.

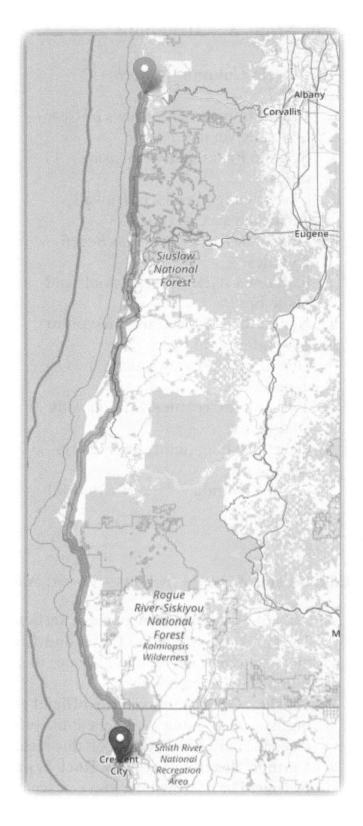

2. Continue for 10 miles and pass through **Waldport, OR**, crossing the Alsea Bay Bridge.
3. Proceed another 15 miles to reach **Yachats, OR**, a small coastal town known for its tidepools and charming main street.
4. Stay on US-101 as the road enters the **Cape Perpetua Scenic Area**; expect winding roads and elevated ocean views.
5. Drive 20 more miles to **Florence, OR**, where you cross the Siuslaw River Bridge. This is a good spot for fuel, food, or a visit to **Old Town Florence**.
6. Continue 47 miles south through the **Oregon Dunes National Recreation Area**, passing through **Reedsport**, **Winchester Bay**, and **North Bend**.
7. Cross the Coos Bay Bridge into **Coos Bay, OR**, the largest coastal city on this stretch.
8. Proceed south 27 miles to **Bandon, OR**, a must-stop destination known for **Face Rock State Scenic Viewpoint** and its rocky shoreline.
9. Drive another 75 miles through small coastal towns like **Langlois**, **Port Orford**, and **Gold Beach**, where you'll cross the **Rogue River Bridge**.
10. Continue following US-101 south along dramatic cliffs and forest-lined curves for another 35 miles until you enter **Brookings, OR**, the last major Oregon town.
11. From Brookings, it's just 6 more miles before crossing into **California**, and shortly after you'll arrive in **Crescent City, CA**, ending Day 2.

Campground	Location	Miles from Newport	Notes
Carl G. Washburne State Park	North of Florence, OR	20	Coastal forest setting, close beach access
Jessie M. Honeyman State Park	Florence, OR	26	Popular for sand dunes and lake activities, full hookups
Bullards Beach State Park	Bandon, OR	87	Spacious RV sites near Bandon's beaches
Harris Beach State Park	Brookings, OR	150	Oceanfront with full RV amenities, ideal last stop before CA

Scenic Stop / Attraction	Location	Miles from Newport	Highlights
Cape Perpetua Scenic Area	Yachats, OR	24	Clifftop hikes and crashing surf views
Sea Lion Caves	North of Florence	32	Largest sea cave and wild sea lions

Heceta Head Lighthouse	Florence, OR	35	Historic lighthouse with a trail and coastal views
Oregon Dunes Overlook	Reedsport, OR	50	Dramatic dunes and forested overlooks
Face Rock Viewpoint	Bandon, OR	90	Photography spot with sea stacks
Samuel H. Boardman Scenic Corridor	Brookings, OR	160	Short trails and stunning cliff-side views

Fuel Station	Location	Miles from Newport	Notes
Chevron Florence	Florence, OR	26	Convenient just off US-101, RV access
Shell Coos Bay	Coos Bay, OR	75	Full-service with food and restrooms
Chevron Bandon	Bandon, OR	90	Good turnaround point for RVs
76 Station Brookings	Brookings, OR	150	Final refuel before entering California

Hidden Facts & Cool Discoveries

- **Cape Perpetua is home to a natural phenomenon called "Thor's Well"**, a collapsed sea cave that appears to drain the ocean. It's most dramatic during high tide — but beware, it's dangerous to approach too closely.
- **The Sea Lion Caves is the largest sea cave in North America.** It's not just a tourist stop — it's a wild, protected habitat where hundreds of Steller sea lions live year-round. You take an elevator 200 feet down into the cave.

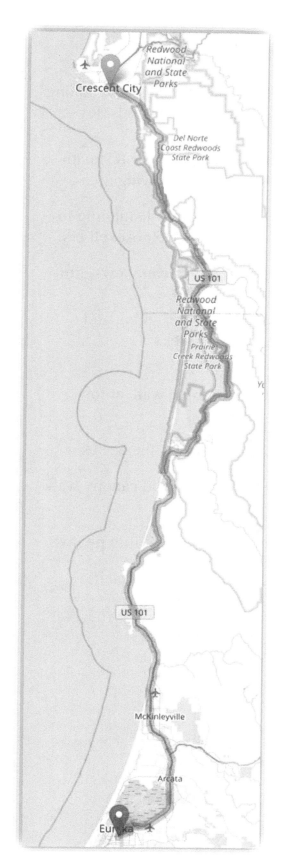

Day 3 – U.S. Highway 101 (Crescent City, CA → Eureka, CA)

Distance: ~85 miles
Estimated Driving Time: ~3 hours (without stops, more with scenic detours)

1. Start in **Crescent City, CA**, heading south on U.S. Highway 101 from the central downtown area.
2. Drive for approximately 3 miles and pass by **Battery Point Lighthouse**, visible at low tide.
3. Continue on US-101 south for 5 miles and enter the **Redwood National and State Parks** region.
4. Take the **Newton B. Drury Scenic Parkway** exit (right) for a 10-mile detour through an old-growth redwood forest. Follow signage and rejoin US-101 at the southern end.
5. Continue 8 miles south to reach **Klamath, CA**. Optional stop at the **Tour Thru Tree** or **Klamath River Overlook**.
6. Proceed another 5 miles to **Trees of Mystery**, a roadside attraction featuring towering redwoods, a canopy walk, and a massive Paul Bunyan and Babe the Blue Ox statue.
7. Stay on US-101 south for 18 miles to **Orick, CA**, a gateway to **Prairie Creek Redwoods State Park** and the **Elk Meadow** area — keep an eye out for Roosevelt elk grazing near the road.
8. Continue another 23 miles south on US-101 to **Trinidad, CA**, a picturesque seaside village known for its harbor, memorial lighthouse, and beach trail access.
9. From Trinidad, drive the final 23 miles on US-101 to enter **Eureka, CA**.
10.   Arrive in downtown Eureka, where you can explore **Old Town Eureka**, **Carson Mansion**, and the **Humboldt Bay waterfront** to end your day.

Campground Name	Location	Distance from Crescent City	Notes
Jedediah Smith Redwoods State Park	Near Crescent City	~2 miles	Riverside campground among old-growth redwoods. RV-friendly.
Kamp Klamath RV Park & Campground	Klamath, CA	~23 miles	Full hookups, near Klamath River & elk viewing areas.
Elk Prairie Campground (Prairie Creek Redwoods SP)	Orick, CA	~42 miles	No hookups, but stunning location among Roosevelt elk.
Patrick's Point SP (now Sue-meg State Park)	Trinidad, CA	~62 miles	Forest and ocean views, limited RV sites.
Mad River Rapids RV Park	Arcata/McKinleyville	~75 miles	Full amenities, pool, and close to Eureka.

Name	Location	Description
Battery Point Lighthouse	Crescent City	Tidal-access lighthouse; picturesque walk at low tide.
Klamath River Overlook	Near Klamath	Panoramic views of the river meeting the ocean.
Trees of Mystery	Klamath, CA	Iconic roadside attraction with redwood canopy walk and Paul Bunyan statue.
Elk Meadow	Prairie Creek SP	Common elk grazing area; great for wildlife photos.
Trinidad Head	Trinidad	Short scenic hike with 360° views of the Pacific Ocean.

Station Name	Location	Amenities
Chevron – Crescent City	879 US-101	Diesel, snacks, easy pull-through.
Klamath River Gas	Klamath, CA	Small station, tight for big rigs.
Shell – Orick	121490 US-101	Convenient, but limited maneuvering space.
Chevron – Trinidad	Patrick's Point Dr	RVer-accessible, clean restrooms.
Costco Gas – Eureka	Wabash Ave	Cheapest fuel in the area; large vehicle lanes.

Things to See or Do

- **Drive Newton B. Drury Scenic Parkway**: A detour from US-101 through 10 miles of towering redwoods in Prairie Creek Redwoods State Park.
- **Visit the Tour Thru Tree**: Near Klamath, you can literally drive your RV (if not oversized) through a living redwood.
- **Carson Mansion in Eureka**: A stunning example of Victorian architecture, not open to public inside but worth a stop for photos.
- **Old Town Eureka**: Quaint waterfront district with shops, art, and views over Humboldt Bay.

The End of the Road... For Now

- You've just explored a curated collection of America's most legendary highways— from the vibrant murals of the Mississippi River towns to the towering redwoods of the Pacific Northwest, the coral-lined shores of the Florida Keys, and the dramatic switchbacks of the Beartooth Highway.
- This atlas wasn't designed to simply get you from point A to point B. It was made for those who believe that the journey itself is the destination. The pages you've flipped through are not just maps—they are invitations. To stop. To look. To breathe in the silence of a canyon. To watch the sun dip behind the sea from your RV window. To take the detour you never planned.
- Whether you followed the Great River Road across the heart of the country, cruised the bends of the Skyline Drive, or chased Pacific fog along US Highway 101, we hope this guide brought ease, clarity, and inspiration to your travels. Every scenic stop, campground tip, and fuel station listed here was chosen to make your adventure richer and smoother—so that your time on the road could focus on connection, not confusion.
- And while you've reached the end of this volume, the road is far from over.

Leave a Review. Help Other Travelers.

- If this book helped you on your journey, inspired a future trip, or simply gave you peace of mind while navigating unfamiliar roads, we'd love to hear your thoughts. **Please consider leaving a quick review on Amazon**—your feedback helps other RV travelers discover this resource and supports future updates and new editions. Even just a few lines make a difference.

What's Next?

- This atlas is part of a growing series celebrating scenic RV travel. Future editions may include expanded routes, reader-submitted favorites, hidden gems, and more U.S. and Canadian highways. Keep your eye on the road—and our upcoming releases.
- Wherever your next adventure takes you—whether it's a spontaneous weekend getaway or a cross-country trek—may your tank be full, your spirit curious, and your camera ready.
- See you on the road.

Made in the USA
Coppell, TX
13 June 2025